TOKYO DISNI

Unlocking the Secrets of Japan's Happiest Place

Roy S. Bowers

Copyright (c) 2024 Roy S. Bowers

All rights reserved. No part of this book may be reproduced in any form by an electronic or mechanical means, including information on storage and retrieval systems, without the permission of the publisher, except by a reviewer who may quote brief passages in a review.

TABLE OF CONTENTS

INTRODUCTION TO TOKYO DISNEY RESORT 7

IS TOKYO DISNEY RESORT WORTH VISITING?. 13

THE BASICS OF VISITING TOKYO DISNEY (Everything you need to know) 16

    How to Buy Disneyland and Disneysea Tickets While Saving Money on Them 16

    Visa Requirements - Your dream of visiting Tokyo Disney Resort is valid… 19

    How To Book Flights to Japan (The most cost-effective and convenient options) 26

    Once you've got your visa sorted out, the next thing is to book flights 26

    Understanding the Queueing System in Tokyo Disney (Avoid the line and Touring Schedules).... 29

PLANNING YOUR TRIP TO TOKYO DISNEYLAND 33

    Dates and Travel 33

    Packing Essentials 34

        The Basics 35

        In Winter 39

        In Summer 40

        In Rainy Season 41

Best Time to Visit (Crowd Calendar) 43
   Best Time to Visit 44
   Worst time to Visit 44
Number Of Days to Spend 45
Park Tickets... 45
Food 52
   Ways to Save Money on meals 55
Restaurants 56
Money Needs 59
Merchandise and Souvenirs 62
   Ways to Save Money on Souvenirs at Tokyo Disney 63
Wi-Fi, Sim Card, and Pocket Wi-Fi 64
HOW TO GET TO TOKYO DISNEY RESORT 70
   By Train 70
   By Bus 71
   By Airport Shuttle 72
WHERE TO STAY (SELECTING A LODGING OPTION)... 74
English Language at Tokyo Disneyland 82
   Japanese short phrases 82
   Cultural Differences 86

What Distinctions Does Tokyo Disneyland Have from Walt Disney World? 87

Tokyo Disney Resort Popular Theme Areas 93

Exploring The Parks Best Rides 98

For Thrill-Seekers 100

For Fantasy Fans 101

For The Whole Family 102

Enchanted Adventures 104

FANTASY SPRINGS 105

Fantasy Springs Overview 106

Accessing Fantasy Springs 106

Fantasy Springs Entrance 107

Tokyo DisneySea Fantasy Springs Hotel 108

TOKYO DISNEY SPECIAL SHOWS AND PARADES 110

Beyond the parks 117

Ikspiari 121

How to Optimize Your Tokyo Disneyland Trip 124

GUESTS WITH DISABILITIES 129

Tokyo Disney Resort's Disability Access Service (DAS) Explained 131

Who is eligible for a DAS pass at Tokyo Disney Resort? 132

How to use the DAS pass at Tokyo Disney
Resort:... 133
Does the DAS pass cost money?....................... 135
CONCLUSION... 136

INTRODUCTION TO TOKYO DISNEY RESORT

Hop on a ride with me as I take you on a scintillating trip to one of the world's best theme parks - Tokyo Disney Resort.

I promise it won't be boring...

Ready?

Imagine a place where magic comes alive, where childhood dreams dance around every corner, and where laughter fills the air like the scent of freshly baked cake.

This is Tokyo Disney Resort, a world like no other, where the iconic stories of Disney come alive in a vibrant tapestry of rides, shows, and delectable treats.

Nestled at Urayasu, Chiba Prefecture, Japan near Tokyo. Tokyo Disney Resort, houses Tokyo Disneyland, a magical theme park, and DisneySea, a unique theme park inspired by the myth and legends of the sea.

It is a magical place where you will experience the enchanting world of Disney's beloved films and characters. Since it's a magical place, it is a popular destination for both locals and tourists.

Its gate is famously adjacent to both Maihama Station and Tokyo Disneyland Station.

Tokyo Disneyland

Tokyo Disneyland was constructed on April 15, 1983, by Wed Enterprises in the same architectural style as Disneyland California and Magic Kingdom in Florida.

Moreso, it was the first Disney Park to be constructed outside the US. It is owned by Oriental Land Company which licenses intellectual property from The Walt Disney Company.

Interestingly, it itself and its companion park; DisneySea, are the only Disney parks in the world not owned by The Walt Disney Company.

Now here's where it gets more interesting…

Whether you are a big fan of classical fairy tales, breathtaking adventures, whimsical cartoons or just seeking a magical escape. Tokyo Disneyland has something for everyone.

Get condensed in sheer joy as you explore the seven lands, each has its attractions, restaurants, and shows. Also enjoy seasonal events, fireworks, and parades that celebrate the spirit of Disney.

Tokyo DisneySea

There are a few Disneylands in the world but are you aware that there is only one DisneySea in the world? You'll find it in Japan.

Tokyo Disney Resort's Tokyo DisneySea is a fantasy theme park exclusive to Japan.

It is motivated by maritime folklore and mythology.

The resort's second park is called Tokyo DisneySea. On September 4, 2001, it opened for 335 billion yen, or roughly US$2.7 billion (about $8 per person in the US). Tokyo DisneySea, the fourth-most visited theme park worldwide, is frequently referred to as the jewel in the Disney Park crown.

This ambitious theme park showcases what is possible when Imagineers are free to explore their imagination, with seven themed ports of call, or lands.

Tokyo DisneySea is appropriate for all ages; however, it was made with an adult audience in mind.

To cater to the strong culinary tastes of Japanese guests, the park offers more table service restaurant options than Tokyo Disneyland and serves alcoholic beverages, which are not accessible at the next park. Just like the name implies, DisneySea is nautical-themed and overlooks Tokyo Bay.

Tokyo Disney Resort is not made up of just one park, but two: Tokyo Disneyland, a classic Disney wonderland brimming with familiar characters and nostalgic rides, and Tokyo DisneySea, a world of mystery and adventure inspired by Disney movies and legends.

The Resort is open for 365 days (about 12 months) of the year except otherwise stated on their website. The only time it closes is for maintenance.

As a result of this, the resort is always filled with people. Tokyo Disneyland had a reported 17. 9 million visitors in

2018 making it the third most popular theme park in the world.

Tokyo DisneySea on the other hand had 14.7 million visitors in the same year, which made it the fourth most popular theme park in the world.

The resort houses nine on-site hotels including three that are run by Disney. It also has a shopping center and a private monorail station.

Although many aspects of the parks may be familiar to regular visitors and fans of Disney-themed parks, there are still many attributes that are unique only to Disney Resort which will make your visit there eventful.

So, if you're looking to visit both parks (Disneyland and DisneySea) or either of them, then this guide has got you covered.

In this guide, we will help you plan your next vacation to Tokyo Disney Resort to ensure you make the most of your magical adventure. We will furnish you with all the secret gems, tips, and tricks on how to book, where to stay, choosing the right time to visit as well as navigating the parks like a pro.

Also, we'll keep you abreast with some of the latest news and updates on the park's attractions and events, including the upcoming Fantasy Springs expansion at Tokyo DisneySea, which will open in June 2024.

Fantasy Springs will be the biggest expansion to any existing theme park ever, featuring 4 new areas based on Frozen, Tangled, Peter Pan, and Aladdin.

If you are interested in embarking on a fun-filled journey to Tokyo Disney, pack your bags, sprinkle on a little pixie dust, and get ready to embark on an unforgettable adventure in the heart of Japan.

Are you prepared to enter a magical world?

Chapter 1

IS TOKYO DISNEY RESORT WORTH VISITING?

Before we get into all the details about visiting Tokyo Disney, let's stop and answer this all-important question, 'is visiting Tokyo Disney worth it?' Shall we?

There is no doubt that the answer to this question is "YES."

The following are some of the reasons visiting Tokyo Disney Resort is worth it;

✅ You will enjoy the best of both worlds at Tokyo Disneyland and DisneySea. Its rides and attractions are even more immersive thanks to a magical fusion of high-tech technologies and the timeless charm of Disney. There are rides in the parks that are exclusive to it and cannot be found anywhere else.

✅ Enchantment and magic: Tokyo Disney is renowned for its immersive atmosphere, capturing the essence of Disney magic with meticulous attention to detail. Expect themed areas, elaborate parades and shows, friendly character interactions, and delicious themed food.

✅ Unique experiences: Tokyo Disneyland and DisneySea offers unique rides and attractions not found in other Disney parks, like Journey to the Mysterious Island and Pooh's Hunny Hunt. These parks also cater to a wider age range with thrill rides alongside gentler and family-friendly options.

✅ Cultural touch: Experience a blend of Disney magic and Japanese culture. Witness stunning castle architecture inspired by Edo-era palaces, enjoy delicious Japanese-inspired snacks, and immerse yourself in the park's impeccable service and hospitality.

✅ Efficiency and convenience: Tokyo Disney Resort is known for its efficiency and well-organized transportation system. Getting to and around the park is easy, and lines tend to move quickly compared to other Disney parks.

✅ Variety: Tokyo Disneyland t of the larger Tokyo Disney Resort, which includes a second park, Tokyo DisneySea, offering a different theme and atmosphere. You can spend multiple days exploring both parks without getting bored.

In essence, if you're a Disney fan, enjoy themed experiences, and embrace cultural immersion then Tokyo Disney Resort can be a truly magical experience.

Chapter 2

THE BASICS OF VISITING TOKYO DISNEY (Everything you need to know)

To ensure a magical and smooth trip to Tokyo Disney Resort, there are a few boxes you need to check to ensure that your planned visit to Tokyo Disney Resort pans out well.

Here's a comprehensive preparation guide:

Let's begin with this one here…

How to Buy Disneyland and Disneysea Tickets While Saving Money on Them

Buying a TICKET for your trip is obvious, isn't it? But let mt me tell you a secret…
Buy your tickets ahead of time! You don't want to buy tickets on D-day.

Quite frankly, you may not even get a ticket if you're visiting during the peak period. Your best bet is to buy your tickets two months before the time of your visit.

Here are some methods for obtaining tickets:

☐ Purchase from Klook - I hear you whisper why Klook? Well, Klook is an online travel agency and the best in Asia. They are an authorized booking partner and on their website are lots of reviews.

When you book with Klook, you do nothing else but just scan the QR code at the entrance. Also, Klook allows you to hit two birds with one stone. Here's what I mean... You can book a convenient one-day or two-day passport to Disney Resort and get to visit both theme parks (Disneyland and DisneySea) without having to pay for different tickets.

Chances are you'll want to experience other brilliant attractions and destinations in Japan. Klook offers tickets for places such as Universal Studios Japan (plus Express Pass), the Ghibli Museum, Sanrio Puroland, and the Robot Restaurant.

☐ Buy via website - Tickets are obtainable via the Tokyo Disney Resort's official website. If you want a way to connect with them directly, you can head over to the resort's official website to book. After booking you can print your tickets at home (which can be changed to a regular-sized ticket for ¥200).

☐ Buy from the Tokyo Disney Resort Tickets Center - Once you arrive at the resort, you can head straight to the Tokyo Disney Resort ticket center on the first floor of Ikspiari.

Date-specific or open Disney tickets?

There are two types of tickets that Tokyo Disney offers: open tickets and date-specific tickets.

Date-specific tickets, which are good for three months (but may vary), ensure your entrance on the date of your choice, regardless of any restrictions.

It is normally preferable to choose the date-specific ticket because you can modify the date on electronic tickets for free (as long as the ticket is still valid).

They can be purchased up to two months in advance.

Does Tokyo Disneyland allow ticket purchases at the gate?

The sales counters at the two Disney theme parks in Tokyo are currently closed. This means you either have to buy online, through a travel agency, an affiliated hotel, or a convenience store within Japan. There can only be five tickets purchased by one group.

Downloading the Tokyo Disney app is highly recommended for convenient access and real-time navigation of the resort and its facilities, regardless of where you purchase your tickets. To book reservations at restaurants and tourist destinations, you'll also need to use the app.

Visa Requirements - Your dream of visiting Tokyo Disney Resort is valid...

Your dream of visiting Tokyo Disney is valid, but you'll probably need to get a visa. There are many different types of Japanese visas which are designed by the Japanese government for different purposes and lengths of time, but you'll only need one of them to visit Tokyo Disney Resort. I'll tell you all about it in a bit.

First, let me fill you in on this important information…

There are over 60 countries whose citizens can enter Japan visa-free for tourism or business.

Currently, to apply for a visa, citizens of other countries must visit a Japanese embassy or consulate. In 2022, Japan launched the e-Visa, which made it easier for US and Canadian individuals to obtain a Japan visa even during periods when pandemic visas were suspended.

Here's a list of the countries that can enter Japan visa-free;

JAPAN VISA-FREE COUNTRIES AND REGIONS			
EUROPE			
Andorra	FYR Macedonia	Lithuania	Serbia
Austria	France	Luxembourg	Slovakia
Belgium	Germany	Malta	Slovenia
Bulgaria	Greece	Monaco	Spain
Croatia	Hungary	Netherlands	Sweden
Cyprus	Iceland	Norway	Switzerland
Czech Republic	Ireland	Poland	United Kingdom
Denmark	Italy	Portugal	

Estonia	Latvia	Romania	
Finland	Liechtenstein	San Marino	
NORTH AMERICA			
Canada	United States		
LATIN AMERICA			
Argentina	Chile	El Salvador	Mexico
Bahamas	Costa Rica	Guatemala	Surinam
Barbados	Dominican Republic	Honduras	Uruguay
ASIA			
Brunei (15 days)	Republic of Korea	Thailand (15 days)	Macao
Indonesia	Singapore	Hong Kong	Taiwan
Malaysia	Qatar		
OCEANIA			
Australia	New Zealand		
MIDDLE EAST			
Israel	United Arab Emirates (30 days)	Turkey	
AFRICA			
Lesotho	Tunisia	Mauritius	

The above-mentioned nationalities are permitted entry for business, tourist, and family visits.

They can stay in Japan for a maximum of 90 days (about 3 months) visa-free and are assigned Temporary Visitor status for limited periods (15 to 90 consecutive days) for tourism or business purposes.

These visitors receive a stamp in their passport which is a requirement for the Japan Rail Pass. The regulations are quite stringent, and obtaining the pass without presenting the stamp is not permitted (visitors holding other forms of visas are not eligible for the pass).

However, visitors cannot be paid for work under Temporary Visitor status. In these situations, obtaining a work visa is required.

If your country doesn't appear on this list, you need a tourist visa to visit Japan.

With that said, here's everything you need to know about Japanese tourist visas…

❖ Japan tourist visa

A Japan tourist visa is a short-term stay visa for sightseeing, visiting friends, or attending conferences or courses. A tourist visa can typically be used for up to 90 days for a single entrance.

Tourists can also apply for a double-entry visa for 2 short trips within 6 months. It is important to note that the Japanese tourist visa does not allow travelers to engage in paid work while in the country.

☼ Japan tourist visa requirements

To successfully apply for a tourist visa to Japan, applicants must meet the following visa requirements:

- Carry a valid passport with two blank pages and at least six months left on it.

- A completed visa application form.

- Present a verified copy of your birth certificate together with a current color passport photo.

- Should you be married, please provide a copy of your marriage license, if it was obtained recently.

- After your permitted stay, you must intend to depart from Japan.

- Evidence of financial capability attesting to your capacity to sustain yourself while visiting Japan.

- Give a bank-issued certificate detailing your financial status for the last six months.
- Submit the applicant's tax return.

- A copy of your Certificate of Employment must be presented if you are applying without a sponsor.

- Give the trip's itinerary and travel schedule.

☀ Japan tourist visa validity

Single-entry visas are valid for 3 months upon the issue and usually allow you to stay in the country for up to 90 days. It is not possible to extend its validity.

Double-entry visas have a validity of 6 months from the date of issue.

Depending on the nationality of the traveler, the reason for the visit, and the type of passport they are carrying, multiple-entry visas often last between one and five years.

Multiple-entry visas allow you to visit Japan multiple times within this period of 1 to 5 years since the issuing date, but each stay cannot exceed the 15 or 30-day period.

☀ Japan tourist visa fees

A fee must be paid to obtain your Japan tourist visa. These fees vary depending on whether you are applying for a single-entry visa, a double-entry, or a multiple-entry visa, as well as on the nationality of the tourist.

Since fees are liable to change at any time, it is a good idea to verify with the local Japanese embassy or consulate before completing your application.

Please be aware that fees are assessed in the local currency of the country where the embassy or consulate is located and must be paid at the time your application is submitted.

Once that has been done, you will receive proof of payment.

☼ Japan Tourist e-Visa

As part of a larger initiative by the government to reach 60 million foreign tourists annually by 2030, a Japan Tourist e-Visa was introduced in August 2022.

Canadian and US nationals could enter Japan without a visa before with the e-Visa, but they can now enter the country without a visa. However, it may be expected to launch for other nationalities in the future.
The online application form will be straightforward to complete which means that tourists do not need to go to an

embassy or consulate to complete the application. Its purpose is to make the application procedure for a visa simpler.

It will be necessary to make a payment by credit or debit card to apply. Once an application has been submitted and approved, the e-Visa approval notice will be sent to applicants by email.

How To Book Flights to Japan (The most cost-effective and convenient options)

Once you've got your visa sorted out, the next thing is to book flights.

Traveling to Tokyo is an exciting adventure, and finding the best flight deal is crucial for a smooth and budget-friendly trip.

Here's a comparison of five popular flight search engines to help you choose the right one for your needs:

Kayak:
Strengths: User-friendly interface, excellent filtering options (including airports, airlines, layovers, and price trends), good for finding deals on domestic and international flights.

Google Flights:
Strengths: Integrated with Google Maps for visualizing flight routes, powerful calendar view for finding the cheapest days to fly, good for discovering alternative airports and nearby destinations.

Skyscanner:
Strengths: Excellent for finding ultra-cheap fares and deals, strong international flight coverage, easy price comparison across airlines and travel agents.

Momondo:
Strengths: Offers a "Metasearch" experience, aggregating results from multiple travel websites and airlines, good for finding hidden gems and unique flight options.

Expedia:
Strengths: One-stop shop for booking flights, hotels, and car rentals, user-friendly interface, offers package deals and rewards programs, often has exclusive deals with airlines.

Choosing the Best Option for Tokyo:

- For finding the best deals: Consider Skyscanner or Momondo for their ability to unearth hidden gems and ultra-cheap fares.

- For user-friendliness and powerful filtering: Kayak or Google Flights offer a smooth experience with comprehensive options for narrowing down your search.
- For package deals and one-stop booking: Expedia might be the ideal choice if you want to combine flights, hotels, and other travel arrangements.

Remember:

- Compare prices across multiple platforms before booking.
- Be flexible with your travel dates, if possible, to score better deals.
- Sign up for price alerts to stay updated on any changes in fares.
- Consider additional factors like baggage fees, layovers, and airline reputation when making your final decision.

◆ **DOWNLOAD THE DISNEY RESORT APP**

Your essential companion! You won't have to worry about anything thanks to this software. It is where you can obtain Standby passes, check wait times, buy Disney premier access, book restaurants, obtain entry passes for certain events, and seamlessly plan your day. Hence, be sure to keep it close by.

Understanding the Queueing System in Tokyo Disney (Avoid the line and Touring Schedules)

There are four passes available at Tokyo Disneyland and they are;

- Entry Request
- Standby Pass
- Disney Premier Access
- (NEW) 40th Anniversary Priority Pass for Tokyo Disney Resort

All four of these passes can be obtained on the Disney Resort App. Now let me explain the function of each one of them.

☐ ENTRY REQUEST - Before you are allowed entry into certain events or experiences, you'd need an entry request. Currently, it is mostly used for characters' meet and greet (not used for rides). Insider tip: They do sell out at times, so what this implies is that you should book as soon as you get in.

☐ STANDBY PASS - This one is used in booking a time to join the queue at certain attractions and shops. Let me explain, when you book a Standby Pass, it will tell you when to return to join the queue for an attraction.

Do you understand?

This increases convenience and makes the queue much shorter and faster for those who obtained Standby passes. But a Standby Pass is not necessarily a requirement. It lessens queues but, on some days, they won't even be released.

On other days, it might be a time when only those who obtained a Standby Pass can join the queue.

You are allowed to hold only one standby pass at a time during your visit. You can obtain another standby pass for a different attraction once you've utilized the one you already have, so use it courteously.

Standby passes are limited in supply and not all the rides require it. However, it does mean that some of the popular rides may require it. These rides could be fully booked for the day and no more standby passes will be issued.

☐ DISNEY PREMIER ACCESS - This was launched in May 2022, and it is a paid FASTPASS. It has a fee of 1500-2500 yen that you must pay in addition to the entrance ticket to be able to join the express queue to some of the most popular rides and even the parades.

The highly spoken about Beauty and the Beast is one of the rides on Disney Premier Access. However, you can only obtain one Disney Premier Access per entrance ticket every hour.

The difference between the Disney Premier access pass and all the passes is that you'll be able to specify which time you want to access the attraction.

☐ (NEW) PRIORITY PASS - The priority pass was introduced to mark the 40th anniversary of Tokyo Disney Resort. It became available on 26 July 2023. It is the newest type of pass available at the Resort. Otherwise called the Disney Resort 40th Anniversary Priority Pass. The name kind of insinuates that it might be temporary but only time will reveal if it's temporary or not.

From my experience and that of others, it works just like the Fast Pass system they used to have. With it, you can reserve a time to come back to certain attractions to skip the queue, but you cannot choose the time. You are also allowed to reserve one Priority Pass every 2 hours. Take note because this too can sell out.

Now that we have gotten this out of the way, the next thing to talk about is planning your trip to Tokyo Disneyland.

Chapter 3

PLANNING YOUR TRIP TO TOKYO DISNEYLAND

Listen to the sweet melody of a Tokyo Disneyland getaway!

I bet you love the sound of this… But before you pack your Mickey ears and hop on a monorail you need to count the cost. It never hurts to have a rough estimate of what you'd be spending.

So, let's talk about dollars and yen. We'll tell you everything you need to know to have a smooth sailing trip.

Here's a breakdown of how to plan your trip…

Proven Ways to Cut Cost while Planning, Travelling, and Sightseeing

Dates and Travel

Decide on your travel dates and book flights and accommodation well in advance, especially during peak seasons. Consider transportation options from the airport like trains or Disney Resort Line monorail.

Packing Essentials

Deciding what to pack when going on a trip is almost as stressful as deciding when and where to go!

While everyone has their preferences for those day-to-day items you pack like clothes and toiletries, allow me to relieve some of the stress by providing you with a list of items I typically bring with me when I visit Tokyo Disney Resort.

These all contribute to a far more pleasurable day spent in the parks, but many of them depend on the season and weather (don't worry, I've categorized them for you).

Although some things may seem absolutely strange, we can assure you that you will feel more at ease if you bring them.

While you can purchase many of these in advance of your trip, other items—like Daiso Japan—are best purchased on arrival! Our criteria for these items are easy to carry/pack or you can buy in Japan after you arrive.

The Basics

These items are perfect for any time of the year. While some of these are optional, you'll notice many other guests at the parks toting these along.

☐ **Battery Charger** – No matter how long your cell phone battery says it's good to last for, you rarely want to leave your hotel or apartment in Japan without a battery charger.

It not only keeps your phone charged, but it can also charge any other USB-powered gadgets you may have with it, including your pocket Wi-Fi if you are carrying one.

You can purchase this before you depart, or you can wait and purchase a cute Disney one at Loft or Yodobashi Camera in Japan!

☐ **Walking Shoes** – You will do a ton of walking, and nothing makes me cranky faster than terrible shoes. I admire New Balance and firmly believe in their products.

They are incredibly popular in Japan. It is advised that you purchase and break them in before your trip.

☐ **Tote Bag** – You will need a bag to carry all your Tokyo Disney Survival Items with you. I love using a tote bag because it makes everything in your bag accessible quickly and easily.

Also, compared to a backpack, it's quick and easy to stow away when going to attractions.

If you can wait until you arrive at the Resort, you'll be pleasantly surprised with the choice of tote bags at the park stores.

You are guaranteed to find something you like there because they rotate nearly every month. There will be something you like there because they rotate virtually every month.

If you want to save some money, check out the 50% off section at any of the Disney Stores in Japan, which usually have totes bags.

☐ **Refillable Water Bottle** – Keeping hydrated is the difference between a fantastic day to a headache-filled "wish I had drunk more water" type of day.

Bring yourself a nice-sized water bottle and refill it throughout the day. The ideal location for this is the water fountains found inside restaurants since the water is normally colder there. Reuse a plastic water bottle that you already purchased to save some cash.

☐ **Leisure Sheet** – Now, this one may seem a bit strange, but hear me out.

It's common to see people sitting on plastic picnic blanket-style sheets on the ground while they wait for a parade or performance.

These are called "leisure sheets," and local fans of Tokyo Disney Resort really like them. You don't want to sit on the bare ground, do you? You should get a "leisure sheet" from Daiso (or purchase one at the resort) if you don't think so.

It is also perfect for those days when it is raining too.

☐ **Plastic Folder for Park Maps** – Instead of stuffing your pack maps into your pocket or bag and then finding them in a crumpled mess, put them in a plastic folder! You can find these at Daiso (they sometimes carry Disney-themed ones) or right at the resort.

I used to think it was silly, but I found it made life easier when I did not have to fight with trying to pull the park map out of my bag.

☐ **Body Wipes** – Body Wipes: You will sweat out throughout the year. If you are spending the entire day at the resort, sometimes you want to freshen up. They smell like everything from citrus to rose petals. Grab some body wipes at Daiso or 7-11.

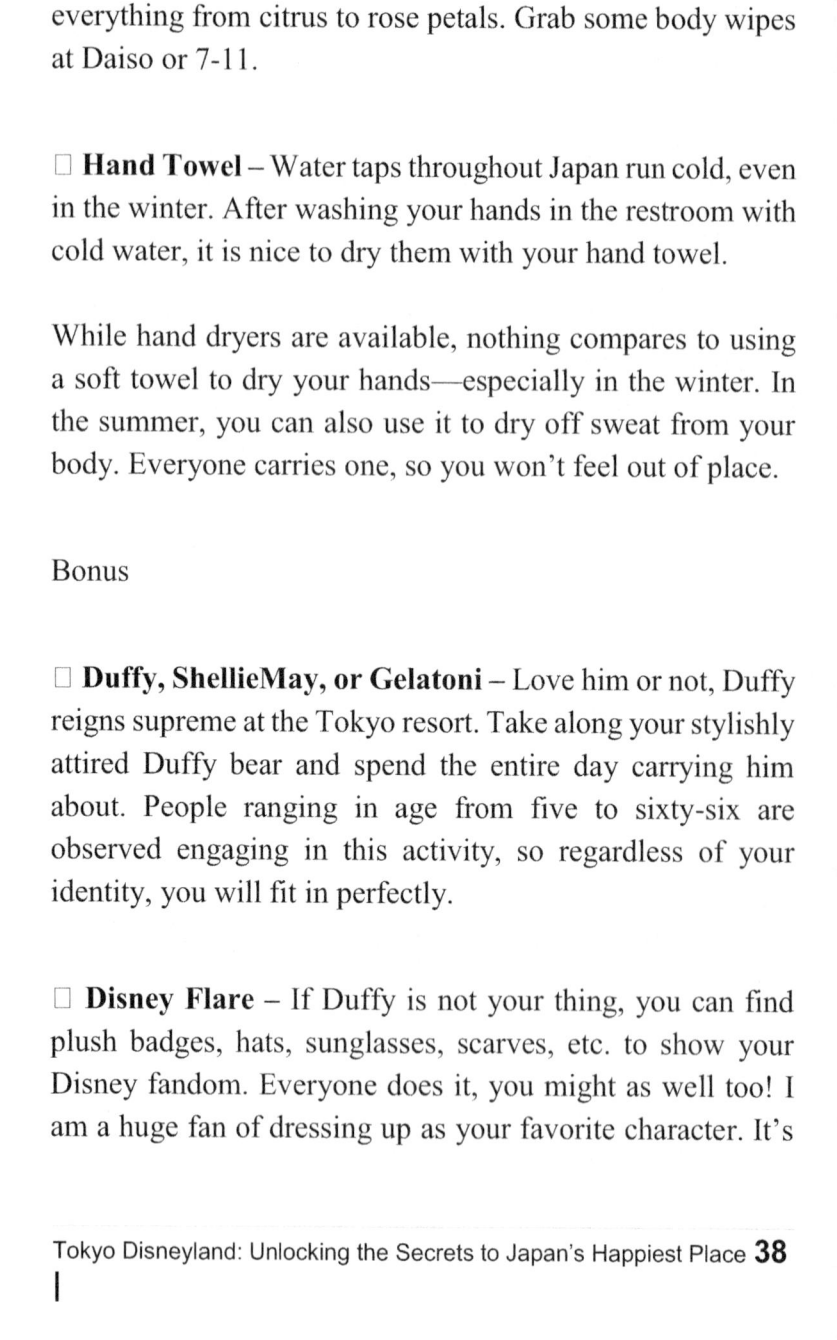

☐ **Hand Towel** – Water taps throughout Japan run cold, even in the winter. After washing your hands in the restroom with cold water, it is nice to dry them with your hand towel.

While hand dryers are available, nothing compares to using a soft towel to dry your hands—especially in the winter. In the summer, you can also use it to dry off sweat from your body. Everyone carries one, so you won't feel out of place.

Bonus

☐ **Duffy, ShellieMay, or Gelatoni** – Love him or not, Duffy reigns supreme at the Tokyo resort. Take along your stylishly attired Duffy bear and spend the entire day carrying him about. People ranging in age from five to sixty-six are observed engaging in this activity, so regardless of your identity, you will fit in perfectly.

☐ **Disney Flare** – If Duffy is not your thing, you can find plush badges, hats, sunglasses, scarves, etc. to show your Disney fandom. Everyone does it, you might as well too! I am a huge fan of dressing up as your favorite character. It's also a great chance to show off the fantastic pin lanyard you collect if you're a regular at the US parks.

In Winter

Winter in Japan is cold compared to where the US Parks are located.

You may find yourself quite shocked if you are from a warmer climate. Even for those from colder climates, it is still a good idea to pack some of these items, you won't be sorry.

☐ **HeatTech Undershirt** – Uniqlo has this amazing undershirt called HeatTech which helps hold your body heat. It fits under everything you are wearing perfectly because it is light and thin.

These are a must if you happen to be coming in the winter.

If you find yourself visiting in the winter, these are a must. Conversely, if you already have Under Armour heat gear, this is a perfect place to layer up with it.

☐ **Hand Warmers** – Taking your gloves off and on constantly is a hassle. Pick up these small disposable hand warmers and never have cold fingers again.

They feel amazing inside the pockets of your jacket while waiting for the next showing of Tokyo Disneyland Electrical Parade Dream lights. During the winter months, these are available everywhere, including Daiso.

☐ **Shoe Warmers** – These are like hand warmers but for your shoes! I used to think these were silly and unnecessary, but after slipping them into my shoes on a cold day I can never go back. Nothing worse than cold toes.

In Summer

Summertime in Japan is hot and humid, much like the heat in Florida. I always carry these few items with me, and you ought to do as well.

Not only do they help keep you cool, but they also help keep you safe in the heat;

☐ **Cooling Towel:**

Aside from a water bottle, if you only bring one item with you in the summer, make it a cooling towel. Even when the towel gets wet, this amazing technology keeps you cool. You can resume using it when it dries by simply soaking it in cold water once more. I suggest purchasing the more costly versions online as they are available through the Disney Store. That way you have them with you as soon as you land.

☐ **Cooling Pad** – These little pads stick to your body and keep you cool for hours on end.

While they are small, they are perfect to apply to various areas of your body. For example, the back of your neck or your forehead (though applying it there in public can make you look a little dumb; use the cooling cloth for that). Once more, it's one of those strange things, but I promise you won't regret buying it.

☐ **Cooling Spray** – Take this spray and apply it to your clothes or towel to help cool yourself off instantly. It doesn't get you wet as the towel can, even though it only lasts a minute or two.

☐ **Sun Protection:** Don't forget sunscreen, sunglasses, and a hat, especially during hot summer months.

In Rainy Season

In Japan, rain can come about in a gentle mist or a torrential downpour that lasts for days. There are a few strategies to stay dry in the parks because getting wet will ruin your day.

☐ **Poncho** – Bring a poncho on rainy days. If you're visiting during the rainy season in June, bring a pack of your luggage. You can pick them up at any store or in the parks if you find that the weather changes significantly while you are there.Note that park ponchos are pricey.

☐ **Umbrella** – Everyone uses umbrellas when it rains here, and sometimes it will rain for hours. Best pick up a cheap clear plastic one from Daiso or any convenience store for about ¥500. If you love umbrellas and don't mind spending a bit of money on them, we have a favorite Disney-themed one you might want to get and take home with you!

Where to Buy

Many of these items are available throughout Japan. Convenience stores such as 7-11, Lawson, and FamilyMart carry many of the items on this list.Daiso, also known as the 100 yen shop, is Japan's equivalent of the dollar store with locations all across the country. The closest Daiso to Tokyo Disney Resort is in Shin-Urayasu, which is one train stop away.

Lockers

There are plenty of storage lockers outside Maihama station as well as inside and outside the parks if you don't feel like taking anything with you all day.

Although park lockers tend to fill up faster than outside ones, they do offer quick access in case the weather unexpectedly changes, and you need to grab something!

You will be in great shape to enjoy the parks while being comfortable if you follow this packing list.

Best Time to Visit (Crowd Calendar)

Selecting the ideal time to visit the resort is the hardest task. The most important aspect of your vacation planning is deciding when to visit Tokyo Disneyland, therefore you don't want to make any mistakes.

Before visiting you'd like to consider a few things such as the weather, crowds, and special events.

This is an overview of all the things you should think about:

Best Time to Visit

For pleasant weather and moderate crowds, you may want to consider shoulder seasons like late May just in time for the blooming cherry blossoms, and October-November for the Halloween and Christmas events.

Tuesday through Thursday are often the best days to visit. To verify your dates, use the Tokyo Disneyland Crowd Calendar. Check ride closures to see if you need to change your dates (check using the resort's website).

Worst time to Visit

Fantasy Springs in DisneySea opens on June 6, 2024; expect high crowds from June through the summer.

Avoid peak seasons like Golden Week, weekends, and New Year.

School holidays and national holidays are two more busy seasons. In Japan, school holidays occur from mid-March through early April, late July through August, and late December to early January.

Number Of Days to Spend

The number of days to spend depends on you.

I suggest three days if it's your first time to take advantage of everything the hotels and parks have to offer. You can opt for two days if that's your preference, one day for each park. But ideally, three days or more is enough to make a lasting impression.

In addition, events at Tokyo Disneyland and Tokyo DisneySea change with the seasons and sometimes in between. You have a different experience when you visit in December as opposed to May. All the more reason to visit multiple times!

Park Tickets

Tickets always go on sale three months in advance online and like I mentioned earlier, you'll want to grab yours early. Having said that, here's how much each one costs;

☐ A Tokyo Disneyland Passport or a one-day pass;

- It costs ¥7,400 to ¥10,900 for adults ages (18 - 64) (roughly $68 to $82)

- For kids aged 4-11, it costs ¥4,800 to ¥9000 ($44 to $82).

- For (65+) year olds, it will cost ¥6,800 ($60).

- Toddlers of three years old and younger can enter Tokyo Disneyland for free.

Also, note that prices vary depending on the day of the week and season. Secondly, these tickets are one-park, one-day. You cannot jump parks with it.

☐ The Two-day Passport;

- For adults (18+) it costs ¥13,200 ($120).
- Adolescents (12-17) ¥11,600 ($105).
- Child (4-11) ¥8,600 ($78).

These tickets are meant for one park per day. You cannot visit both parks with it on the same day.

However, you can choose which park you visit on each day (plus you can choose the same park two days in a row). Although there is an exception for Disney Hotel guests as you'll see later on.

☐ The Three-day Magic Passport;

- For adults (18+) ¥17,800 ($161).
- Adolescents ages (12-17) ¥15,500 ($141).
- Child (4-11) ¥11,500 ($104).

These passports function like a two-day passport in the sense that for the first two days, you won't be allowed to jump parks (and yes you can visit the same park two days in a row).

But on the third day, you are allowed to park hop to the fullest.

☐ The Four-day Magic Passport;

- For adults (18+) ¥22,400 ($203).
- For Adolescents between ages (12-17) ¥19,400 ($176).
- For children between ages (4-11) ¥14,400 ($131).

Just like the 3-day passport, these passports function like the 2-day passport where you are not allowed to move between parks in the first two days (again you are permitted to visit the same park two days in a row if you wish to).

Then on the third and fourth day, you are allowed to park hop as you like.

☐ Starlight Passport;

- For adults (18+) ¥5,400 ($49).
- For Adolescents between ages (12-17) ¥4,700 ($43).
- For children between ages (4-11) ¥3,500 ($32).

This passport allows holders passage into either park after 3:00 pm on weekends and national holidays. See the resort's official website for days this is available for sale.

☐ After-6 Passport;

All ages ¥4,200 ($38).

This passport allows holders passage into either park after 6:00 pm on weekdays. See the resort's official website for days this is available for sale.

☐ Two-park Annual Passport;

- Adolescents/Adults (12-64) ¥89,000 ($808).

- For children between ages (4-11) ¥56,000 ($508).

- For seniors ages (65+) ¥75,000 ($681).

For one year after a successful purchase, this passport allows for nearly unlimited access to both Disneyland and DisneySea. This ticket breaks even after 12 days at the park for adults.

But please note that they are blackout days, which are announced nearly a year in advance. When announced, the list of blackout dates are usually available on the resort's official website.
Also, annual tickets are obtainable at the Tokyo Disney Resort Ticket Center on the first floor of the Ikspiari or at the East Gate of Tokyo Disneyland.

☐ One-park Annual Passport;

- Adolescents/Adults (12-64) ¥61,000 ($554).
- For children between ages (4-11) ¥39,000 ($354).
- For seniors ages (65+) ¥51,000 ($463).

For one year after a successful purchase, this allows for near-unlimited access to either Tokyo Disneyland or DisneySea. The ticket breaks even after about 8 days for adults.

It is also important to note that they are blackout days, which are announced nearly a year in advance. When announced, the list of blackout dates are usually available on the resort's official website.

Annual tickets are obtainable at the Tokyo Disney Resort Ticket Center on the first floor of the Ikspiari or at the East Gate of Tokyo Disneyland.

☐ Special Magic Passport;

- Two days for adults (18+) ¥14, 800 ($134).
- Adolescents (12-17) ¥12,800 ($116).
- Children (4-11) ¥9600 ($87).

- Three days for adults (18+) ¥19,400 ($176).
- Adolescents (12-17) ¥16,700 ($152).

- Children (4-11) ¥12,500 ($113).

  - Four days for adults (18+) ¥24,000 ($218).
  - Adolescents (12-17) ¥20,600 ($187).
  - Children (4-11) ¥15,400 (140).

This type of passport is available only to Disney Hotel guests at their front desk. For a small increase of ¥1000 over regular Multi-Day passports, you can park jump from the first day.

☐ Discount Passport;

Discounts are rarely offered and when they are, it is mostly during off-seasons. They are deals available in Japanese convenience stores generally, either for students or locals/visitors to certain areas.

These discounts are about ¥500 ($4) less than what you'd normally pay at the parks.
☐ **OPENING HOURS**

Opening hours vary by season, typically, it is from the hours of 8 am to 10 pm.

Admission ends one hour before closing time. All year long, one can visit the park.

However, be informed that there'll be a temporary closure of the park facilities from 2024/4/8 - 2024/5/10 as announced on the resort's official website.

Food

You probably might be asking, what if all the food is expensive and not good?

Well, there's no cause for alarm... Once you're inside the park, you'll discover that your fears were unfounded.

Now here's the thing...

Tokyo Disneyland offers a bunch of options from quick service meals to a character dining experience.

In addition, your average counter-service meal will run you about $9-$15, and table service sets go up to $90 at their highest, although they generally hover between $20-$50.

These are the "fast food" restaurants where you order at the counter. Some of these places serve standard pizza, fries, and hamburgers.

In addition to quick food, some outlets provide sandwiches, seafood, curries, and Japanese udon. The quality of most counter-service restaurants at both parks outshines that of other Disney Parks in terms of both theming and quality
I recommend budgeting about ¥3000 a day for food if you intend to eat at the parks (enough for two counter-service meals and a snack or two).

For me, here are my favorite meals in Tokyo Disneyland:

1. Three Green Alien Mochi (¥300):

This is seriously THE CUTEST food ever! I squealed when I saw this in person. Three balls of mochi (rice cake) in the shape of the tiny green guys from Toy Story are what they are. Chocolate, custard, and strawberry are the three different fillings for each mochi. Such a genius concept! This is available in Tomorrowland's Plazma Ray's Diner.

2. Mickey Gloves Chicken Sandwich (¥600 a la carte / ¥900 with a set meal):

When I saw it in person, I squealed again. It's a grilled chicken and scrambled eggs sandwich that sounds rather ordinary on the menu. The kicker? It comes in a nicely designed Chinese bun that resembles the gloves of Mickey Mouse! This sandwich is available for purchase at Toontown's Huey, Dewey, and Louie's Good Time Cafe.

3. Mickey-shaped Churros (¥300):

The most well-known churros may have come from the original Disneyland in Los Angeles, but these Mickey-shaped ones are exclusive to Tokyo Disneyland!

I love the subtlety here. The Mickey shape is only visible if you view the churros top down. I might have missed it myself if I didn't know about it! This is present throughout Tokyo Disneyland Park. Simply look out for the candy stand; I found mine at Westernland.

4. Smoked Turkey Leg, a Disneyland Classic! (¥900)
This is a Disneyland classic and a must-have. They tell me it's not as big as the ones in the original Disneyland, but I thought it was perfect! This is available in Westernland at the Cowboy Cookhouse.

Ways to Save Money on meals

1. Before you leave, pick some breakfast from a convenience store. There's a convenience store with a good selection of breakfast items at the Tokyo Disneyland Hotel, which is located directly across the street from the park entrance. An excellent range of hot and ready-to-eat breakfast foods can be found at Maihama Station for a lot less money than what's available at the park.

2. Pack a full day's worth of refreshments and snacks. Drinks in glass bottles or cans, and alcoholic beverages are the only things that are not allowed in the park's picnic sites. Food can be placed in lockers and picked up later.

3. Although meals at Tokyo DisneySea or Disneyland can be a significant aspect of the Tokyo Disney experience, some travelers may find that the meal is not enough in terms of size due to the portion sizes in Japan. The golden rule of picking lunch over dinner—which is always significantly less expensive in Japan—is the solution to this.

4. Check out some restaurant menus beforehand — China Voyager (DL), for example, has bowls of noodles for ¥1,030 while the Dockside Diner (DS) has sets from ¥1,200, which is not bad. At Tokyo Disneyland, Grandma Sara's and the Hungry Bear Restaurant serve reasonable quantities. The set meals are big enough for two people if you do not need to eat much and are about ¥1,500.

Note: To increase your chances of getting a seat at a sit-down restaurant, we strongly advise booking a reservation through the Disney app as early as possible in the morning. The crowds can be much.

In addition, food can be had cheaper at the NewDay's convenience store at JR Maihama Station and pre-made bento boxes are available at the Seijo Ishii grocery store on the first floor of Ikspiari.

When the day is almost over and the food is going to expire, many of those meals are put on sale.

Restaurants

Two restaurants, in particular, hold a special charm: Blue Bayou Restaurant and Captain Hook's Galley.
Let's dive into their unique vibes and tantalizing treats:

Blue Bayou Restaurant:

- Ambiance: Immerse yourself in the romantic elegance of Pirates of the Caribbean. Imagine twinkling lights reflecting off the Pirates of the Caribbean waterway, serenading musicians on a balcony, and lush foliage creating a secluded haven.

- Cuisine: Prepare for a refined dining experience. Savor French-inspired dishes like the signature Monte Cristo sandwich – a delectable creation of ham, turkey, and Swiss cheese dipped in batter and fried to golden perfection. Seafood, pasta, and decadent desserts round out the menu.

- Special Touch: Enhance your experience with a pre-fixe menu featuring multiple courses and a drink or indulge in a prix-fixe menu paired with specially selected wines.

- Reservations: Essential! Blue Bayou is a coveted spot, so book your table well in advance to secure your magical dining experience.

Captain Hook's Galley:
- Ahoy, Mateys! Brace yourself for a pirate-themed adventure! The ship-shaped galley offers an exciting atmosphere with weathered wood, nautical flags, and even a crow's nest lookout.

- Hearty Fare: Fuel up for your swashbuckling adventures with pirate-inspired grub. Think chunky tuna sandwiches, fish and chips, and refreshing buccaneer salads. Don't forget to grab a Mickey-shaped pirate bread or skull bread for a fun snack!

- Casual and Quick: Enjoy a grab-and-go style experience perfect for a break between thrills. Order at the counter and find a spot on the patio or inside the galley to enjoy your pirate grub.

- Budget-Friendly: Captain Hook's Galley is a more affordable option compared to Blue Bayou, making it ideal for families or those on a tighter budget.

Choosing Your Culinary Adventure:

- Romantic Dinner: Blue Bayou's elegant atmosphere and refined cuisine make it ideal for a special occasion or a celebratory meal.

- Family Fun: Captain Hook's Galley's pirate theme and casual setting are perfect for a quick bite with the kids between adventures.

- Taste of Adventure: Enjoy both! Captain Hook's Galley for lunch and Blue Bayou for a memorable dinner date can offer a diverse culinary experience.

Money Needs

Japan is a cash-based society, so having Japanese yen on hand at all times ensures that you won't encounter any issues.

Since many locations don't accept cards, I advise using your card here at the Resort and reserving the cash you converted or withdrew for use throughout the rest of Japan.

A few things to bear in mind are:

- Snack carts are among the several establishments in the resort that accept credit cards.

- Your card must have a signature on the back.

- They might or might not accept your credit card if it doubles as a debit card.

- Carry an extra credit card in case your primary one fails to swipe or function.

- It may take up to a month for certain purchases—such as hotel charges—to show up on your statement.

- To prevent your card from being locked, call your bank and let them know you use it in Japan.

- Cast Members inquire as to how many installments you would like to make for your purchase; this is not customary in North America. By default, they'll ask if you want to make the entire amount at once. They'll gesture with their hands as one. Say "Yes."

Need Some Quick Cash?

On the first floor of Ikspiari, there is a 7-Eleven international ATM if you do need cash. Look for signs near the grocery store and food court.

Only one 7-Eleven ATM exists in the Resort and is in Ikspiari (Tokyo Disney Resort's version of Downtown Disney).
Menus are available in English and other languages. Prior to your travel, don't forget to notify your bank.

How much money should you take out?

Depending on your bank fees, you should withdraw more money to avoid paying more costs if the fees for each transaction are higher.

Budget at least ¥10,000 per person (about $100) for one full day at the parks. This covers snacks, drinks, lunch, supper, and products. It's easy to carry around since there's only one note for ¥10,000.

Does Tokyo International Airport Offer Currency Exchange?

I hear a lot of people asking if they can exchange some cash at the airport, yes you can.

Once at Tokyo International Airport (HND), you can exchange local currency if necessary. Currency exchange is available at the following locations:

- Travelex Terminal 1, First Floor Marketplace, 9 am to 7 pm.

- Haneda Airport Post Office Terminal 1, First Floor Marketplace, open from 9 am to 6 pm, and

- SBJ Bank Terminal 2, First Floor Lobby, 9 am to 7 pm.

Merchandise and Souvenirs

Now and then, seasonal merchandise that needs to be cleared out is put on sale in specially marked areas of shops.

Merchandise can go anywhere from ¥300-¥3500 for most items while for souvenirs you can get classic Disney plush toys to unique Japanese merchandise for about ¥1000 and up ($6.75) for most items.

Ways to Save Money on Souvenirs at Tokyo Disney

1. Make the most of the photo-opportunity areas, e.g. putting your face in a Mickey-shaped hole or striking a pose with a figure is free; you'll receive the pictures and can use the money for something else.

2. Disney Stores throughout Japan, e.g. There are frequently cheap merchandise sections on the third-floor location in Shibuya. Here, you'll find goods that are sometimes only a few months old at 20-70% off the regular price.

3. A "Value Section" is occasionally available at the Bon Voyage Store, which is located on the route from Maihama Station to the resort. This merchandise is discounted up to 50% off.

4. There are deals on merchandise at the park's stores as well. You guessed it—look in the rear and corners of the stores for merchandise bearing red stickers—as these sections aren't really advertised.

5. Nakano Broadway in Tokyo has a secondhand store for Disney merchandise. Save a ton of money by going before your big day!

Here are a few more things to keep in mind as you're planning that may affect your decision:

- The Sindbad's Storybook Voyage will be closed from February 13, 2024, to September 24, 2024.

- Pooh's Hunny Hunt will also be closed from January 26, 2024, until May 24, 2024, for a few months.

- Space Mountain closes permanently after July 31, 2024.

- Fantasy Springs opens on June 6, 2024.

Wi-Fi, Sim Card, and Pocket Wi-Fi

Tokyo Disneyland and Tokyo DisneySea started providing free WiFi in the parks in May 2019.

Recently, SIM cards and mobile hotspots have become easier to obtain in Japan for tourists. Disney Hotels offer complimentary Wi-Fi; for information on other hotels, see their website.

If your phone is unlocked, your best option is a SIM card. There are rental mobile hotspots available for people with carrier-locked phones.

Recommended: Mobal Japan Unlimited 4G Data SIM Card.

Key features are;

- Unlimited Data (throttled to 128 kilobits per second after 7GB)
- No daily limit on data usage.
- Japanese Phone Number.
- Free incoming calls & texts.
- Low-cost outgoing calls.
- Customer service in English (a crucial one for me)
- Choose between a 15- or 30-day trial period of service or ongoing.
- SIM card is nano-sized, but you get a free adapter if you need a different size

The SIM Card itself costs ¥3,000 ($27USD), but they do provide free shipping worldwide; which means you'll need to order this ahead of time and have it mailed to you. Unless you want it transported to your hotel or place of residence in Japan, there is no opportunity to pick it up anywhere.

You activate your SIM card online with the service you want to use after you receive it:

- 15 Day Voice / Text / Unlimited Data: ¥4,000 ($37USD)
- 30 Day Voice / Text / Unlimited Data: ¥6,000 ($56USD)
- Ongoing Voice / Text / Unlimited Data: ¥6,000 per month (¥4,500 or $42USD if you're a student or teacher)
- Ongoing Voice & Text Only: ¥1,000 per month ($9USD)

In most cases, you'll probably choose the 15-day option, which brings the total up to ¥7,000 or about $63USD (SIM card cost + service).

You select the day on which you want the service to begin when you activate your card online (directions are included in your package). Make sure you do this well in advance, as card activation takes about 2 business days.

Recommended: Mobile Wi-Fi Hotspot (7GB)

Product details;

- Upload/ download speed - 4G
- Maximum number of connected devices - 5 devices

- Battery life - 6 hours

- Coverage area - The Whole of Japan

- Traffic flow limit - 7GB

- Local telecom operator - SoftBank

In Japan, you may find free Wi-Fi hotspots in a number of locations:

- Starbucks Japan

- Family Mart (Japanese Only)

OTHER SIM CARD OPTIONS

If your stay in Japan is not intended to last for 15 days, there are less expensive possibilities. Three SIM card choices (data only; no phone number or text messaging) are available from Klook:

- 1GB 4G for 6 Days ($10USD)
- 3GB 4G for 8 Days ($20USD)
- Unlimited 4G for 8 Days ($31USD)

Visit Klook.com for details on how to order. These are available for pickup at Haneda and Narita airports.

By following these tips and tricks you're sure to make the most out of your trip to Tokyo Disney.

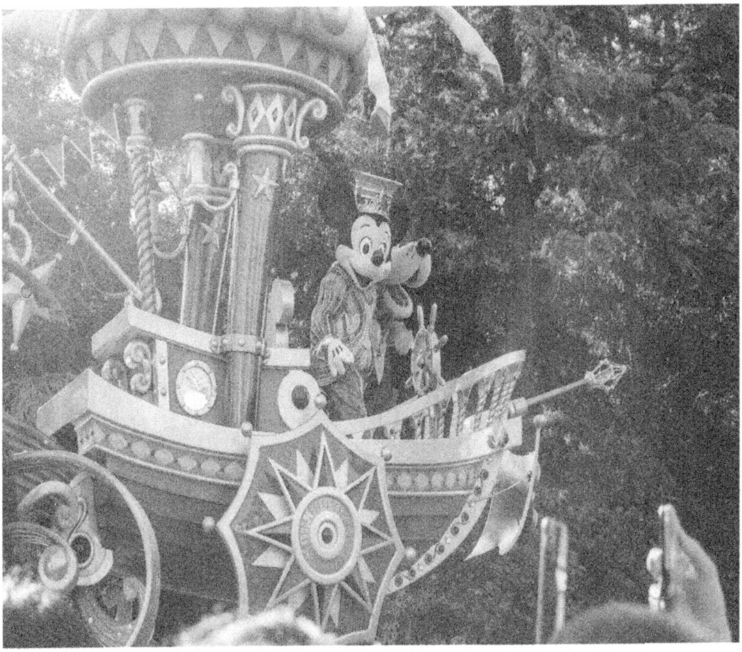

Chapter 5

HOW TO GET TO TOKYO DISNEY RESORT

Getting to Tokyo Disneyland from Tokyo is quite easy and convenient, whether you choose to take the train or the bus.

Tokyo Disney Resort is a five-minute walk from Maihama Station, on the JR Keiyo line.

By Train

Taking the train is the most popular option, offering a comfortable and scenic journey.

The JR Keiyo Line directly connects Tokyo Station with Maihama Station, the station closest to Disneyland. Take the JR Keiyo/Musashino Line from Tokyo Station to JR Maihama Station, which is the sixth stop. The minutes covered is 17 minutes and covered by Japan Rail (JR) pass. The train ticket costs ¥220 without a JR pass.

The train timetable is available online, and tickets can be bought at the station or online.

From Maihama Station, you can walk to Disneyland in about 5-10 minutes, or take the Disney Resort Line monorail for a more magical experience (additional ¥260).

By Bus

Taking the bus is a faster option, especially if you are coming from central Tokyo.

The Tokyo Disneyland Resort Express bus operates directly from several locations in Tokyo, including Shinjuku Station and Tokyo Station.

The ride takes about 1 hour 43 minutes and costs around ¥1000 ($6.75) for a one-way ticket. Tickets can be obtained online or at the bus station.

The bus will drop you off at the Tokyo Disneyland Bus Center, which is a short walk from the park entrance.

By Airport Shuttle

If you'd like to go to Tokyo Disneyland directly from Narita Airport, you can take the Tokyo Disney Resort Bus.

But note that the last bus departs Narita Airport Terminal 1 at exactly 6:10 pm. The journey takes about 1 hour 15 minutes and costs ¥1,800 ($12.15) for adults and ¥900 ($6.08) for children.

At the airport, tickets are available for purchase at the bus ticket counter.

Alternatively, if you have a Japan rail (JR pass), you can use the Narita Express from Narita Airport to Tokyo station.

It is an hour's trip, and from there, take the JR Keiyo line, just like I mentioned above, and get to Tokyo Disneyland in another 15 minutes. The whole transition is about an hour and 15 minutes.

Both Narita Express and the trip by Keiyo line are fully covered by your Japan Rail (JR) pass.

Additional tips and secrets

☐ If you're traveling with a lot of luggage, you may want to take the train, as it's easier to store your bags on the train than on the bus.

☐ If you're on a booth-strapped budget, the bus is the more affordable option.

☐ If you're traveling during peak seasons, it's a good idea to purchase your tickets beforehand, as both the train and bus can get crowded.

Follow these tips to arrive at Tokyo Disneyland safely and without stress.

Chapter 6

WHERE TO STAY (SELECTING A LODGING OPTION)

Ten hotels total—four Disney Hotels and six Official Hotels—are located on the Tokyo Disney Resort territory. Outside of the resort's boundaries are a number of additional Disney-affiliated lodging options, including a few Partner Hotels.

DISNEY HOTELS

For lodging at Tokyo Disney Resort, the Disney Hotels are the most popular and practical options. The perks of staying at a Disney hotel include free monorail passes or shuttle bus rides to and from the parks, free shopping delivery to their room, complimentary shopping delivery to their room, pre-check-in services at JR Maihama Station with baggage delivery, and the ability to purchase park tickets even on days when they are sold out.

Expect the highest level of convenience, added with character greetings and direct access to the park. Immerse yourself in the Disney charm directly inside the park.

But it's quite pricey so be prepared for premium prices.

They include;

☐ Tokyo Disneyland Hotel - Opened in 2008, the Tokyo Disneyland Hotel stands just across from the entrance to Tokyo Disneyland and is designed in an early 20th Century Victorian style. The hotel has shops, restaurants, and an outdoor pool in addition to themed gardens.

☐ Tokyo DisneySea Hotel MiraCosta - The Hotel MiraCosta is the resort's most unique hotel, as it stands partially inside Tokyo DisneySea and offers views into the park from many of its rooms. Additionally, guests get access to a special entry into the park from the hotel and, on some days, are allowed to enter the park slightly earlier than other tourists. The hotel offers spa services, shopping, and restaurants with a theme.

☐ Disney Ambassador Hotel - Another on-site option with a Victorian elegance theme. The first Disney hotel to open in Tokyo Disney Resort was the Disney Ambassador Hotel. It is situated midway between Tokyo Disneyland and Tokyo

DisneySea, near to the Ikspiari shopping center. Hotel facilities include themed restaurants, shops, and a resort-style outdoor pool.

☐ Disney Celebration Hotel - Just a short walk from the park, this value-oriented Disney hotel offers a casual, modern atmosphere with Themed rooms and a fun, budget-friendly experience.

☐ The Toy Story Hotel - Opened in 2022 next to Bayside Station along the monorail. It caters to budget-conscious travelers and is themed after the well-known film series.

OFFICIAL HOTELS

The six Official Hotels are situated on the resort grounds close to the monorail line's Bayside Station.

Benefits for those who stay include free shuttle service from their hotel to Bayside Station, free baggage delivery from JR Maihama Station to their hotel, and the ability to purchase tickets even on days when they are sold out.

They are;

☐ Hilton Tokyo Bay - Situated 0.76km from Tokyo Disneyland. Hilton Tokyo Bay is a luxurious option step away from the Disney Resort Line monorail station. They have spacious rooms, stunning views, multiple restaurants, and a pool. All these options make it a comfortable and convenient choice.

☐ Sheraton Grande Tokyo Bay Hotel - Another high-end choice with bay views, multiple restaurants, a spa, and a fitness center. It is located 0.64km from Tokyo Disneyland, it is near the monorail station, and it offers easy access to the park.

☐ Hotel Okura Tokyo Bay - Experience Japanese elegance with stunning Tokyo Bay views. Relax in the spa, savor delicious cuisines, and enjoy easy access to the park through the monorail.

☐ Tokyo Bay Maihama Hotel - This one is affordable and comfortable; this hotel is a short walk from the monorail station. Simple rooms, multiple restaurants, and a relaxed atmosphere make it good value for budget-conscious travelers.

☐ Tokyo Bay Maihama Hotel First Resort - Family-friendly and casual, with a retro American resort theme. Think bright colors, playful décor, and plenty of activities for kids. It is a 5-minute walk from Tokyo Disneyland and Tokyo DisneySea, with a free shuttle bus service every 10-20 minutes. It has two swimming pools (one indoor, one outdoor).

☐ Grand Nikko Tokyo Bay Maihama - Elegant and luxurious, with a touch of Disney magic. Think spacious rooms, impeccable service, and stunning views of Tokyo Bay. Directly connected to Tokyo DisneySea via a covered walkway, with a 10-minute walk to Tokyo Disneyland. The rooms are refined and modern, with some offering balconies and ocean views. It has a spa, fitness center, indoor pool, several restaurants featuring gourmet Japanese and international cuisine, a Disney shop, and access to exclusive park benefits like priority entry to select attractions.

PARTNER HOTELS

A short drive from the resort is four Partner Hotels, which are situated outside the park grounds. Partner hotel guests can have their bags delivered to their hotel from JR Maihama Station for a minimal cost, and they also benefit from free shuttle bus service to and from the resort.

The benefit of purchasing park tickets is currently not available.

☐ Oriental Hotel Tokyo Bay - Another budget-friendly option with clean rooms, a friendly atmosphere, and a convenient location near the monorail station.

☐ Hotel Emion Tokyo Bay - Sleek and stylish decor, comfortable rooms with panoramic views, ideal for couples or solo travelers. Conveniently connected to DisneySea via a monorail and close to Disneyland by free shuttle. Onsen (hot springs) on-site for soaking and rejuvenation after theme park adventures.

☐ Urayasu Brighton Hotel Tokyo Bay - Fun and vibrant atmosphere, themed rooms, kids' club with activities, and a rooftop pool with city views. Just a 10-minute walk to either Disneyland or DisneySea, providing easy access to the magic. Buffet restaurants and cafes offer convenient and affordable meal options.

☐ Mitsui Garden Hotel Prana Tokyo Bay - Modern rooms with soothing decor, indoor bathhouse with ocean views, perfect for unwinding after a day at the parks. Massage services, a fitness center, and a spacious lobby bar provide options for leisure and socializing. Regular shuttle buses to both Disneyland and DisneySea, ensuring convenient park access.

In conclusion, the best hotel for you will depend on your budget, priorities, and desired level of Disney immersion.

With so many excellent options near Tokyo Disneyland, you're sure to find the perfect place to stay for your magical adventure!

Tokyo Disneyland: Unlocking the Secrets to Japan's Happiest Place **81**

Chapter 7

English Language at Tokyo Disneyland

I know you probably would be asking if they speak English at Tokyo Disney.

Yes, they do speak English here. Both park employees and cast members speak English and other languages.

But it is important to note that the English-speaking members aren't always available. For the convenience of all, the majority of the signage within the park is multilingual.

However, you can make the most of your vacation if you can master a few simple Japanese phrases. It is like adding that extra layer of flavor to your adventure sundae.

Japanese short phrases

The following are useful expressions to remember:

Greetings and Essentials:

- Hello (good afternoon) - Konnichiwa (こんにちは) Pronunciation: kohn-nee-chee-wah

- Arigatou gozaimasu: Thank you - (ありがとうございます)
  Pronunciation: ah-ree-gah-toh goh-zah-ee-mahs

- Sumimasen: Excuse me - (すみません)
  Pronunciation: su-mi-ma-sen

- Onegaishimasu (お願いします)、please.
  Pronunciation: o-ne-gai-shi-masu

- Doitashimashite: You're welcome - (どういたしまして)
  Pronunciation: do-i-ta-shi-ma-shi-te

At the Park:

- [Attraction name] ni narabi masu ka?: May I line up for [attraction name]? - [アトラクション名に並びますか？]
  Pronunciation: a-to-ra-ku-shon mei ni na-ra-bi ma-su ka?

- FastPass o onegaishimasu: May I have a FastPass, please? - [ファストパスをお願いします] Pronunciation: fasu-to-pasu o o-ne-gai-shi-masu

- Toire wa doko desu ka?: Where is the restroom? - [トイレはどこですか?] Pronunciation: to-i-re wa do-ko desu ka?

- Mizu o onegaishimasu: May I have some water, please? -- [水をください] Pronunciation: mi-zu o kudasai

- Kore o kudasai: Can I have this, please? - (pointing to the desired item) - [これください] Pronunciation: ko-re ku-da-sai

Character Interactions:

- [Character name] ni Yamashita desu: I would like to meet [character name]. - [キャラクター名に会いたいです] Pronunciation: kyara-ku-ta-a me ni ai-tai desu

- Issho ni shashin o tora sete kudasai: Can we take a picture together, please? - [一緒に写真を撮らせてください] Pronunciation is-sho ni sha-shin o to-ra-sa-se-te ku-da-sai

General Politeness:

- Hajimemashite: Nice to meet you -[はじめまして] Pronunciation: ha-ji-me-ma-shi-te

- Gochisousama deshita: The food was delicious (after eating) - [ごちそうさまでした] Pronunciation: go-chi-sou-sama de-shi-ta

- Otsukaresama desu: You must be tired (to someone working hard) - [お疲れ様です] Pronunciation: o-tsu-ka-re-sama desu

Bonus:

- Kawaii!: Cute! - [かわいい!] Pronunciation: ka-wa-i-i!

- Ganbatte!: Good luck! - [がんばって!] Pronunciation: gan-bat-te!

To wrap up remember, even a few simple phrases can make a big difference. The effort to learn some Japanese will be appreciated by the staff and make your interactions with locals more enjoyable.

I hope this list helps you with your magical adventure!

Cultural Differences

Traveling to a foreign country comes with experiencing first-hand cultural differences. Tokyo Disney Resort has some unique practices, even for seasoned Disney visitors. You'll quickly notice the following cultural differences:

- Smaller portion sizes for most food items. In general, Japanese people consume smaller portions than people in the West. You may find yourself eating more often simply because of this.
- Guests are typically quiet at attractions. This includes thrill rides. Even though your guests will laugh and shout with delight, it's normal if the majority of them are as silent as a mouse in the car.
- Parades are usually best enjoyed while seated; in certain cases, you have to sit for the entire performance. Bring your leisure sheet, snacks, and

favorite distractions, and get cozy while you wait for the next parade!
- Refrain from giving the salesperson your credit card or cash when paying for an item or after a meal until they extend their hand. Place your cash or credit card in the tiny dish provided. To be picked up by you, the cashier will place your card, change, and receipt in the dish. This is true for Japan as a whole as well as the resort.
- It's not typical at the resort or in Japan to customize your meal. You will get the tomato if the cheeseburger is served with one. Asking for customization can cause unneeded confusion. It's simpler to change your order once you've sat down at your table, unless you have an allergy.

What Distinctions Does Tokyo Disneyland Have from Walt Disney World?

Tokyo Disneyland first opened its gates in 1983 and was the first Disney Park to open outside of the United States.

Tokyo DisneySea, a second park next to Tokyo Disneyland, opened its doors in 2001.

These two parks are the only parks in the world to not be owned or operated by the Walt Disney Company, and license intellectual property from them instead. However, this doesn't make Tokyo Disneyland any less magical.

Tokyo Disneyland is regarded by some as the pinnacle of Disneyland and Disney World merged into one amusement park.
Disneyland Tokyo looks a lot like Disney World from the outside. Both parks have the same version of Cinderella Castle, versions of Main Street, and the iconic four "lands".

However, there are several major differences between Tokyo Disneyland and Walt Disney World.

☐ World Bazaar

Upon entry to Walt Disney World, you are greeted with the iconic Main Street USA. Tokyo Disneyland has its version of this entryway known as the World Bazaar.

Because it is based on America in the early 20th century, the area has a very similar appearance to Main Street USA. The major difference is that the World Bazaar is covered with a glass canopy ceiling which is helpful for bad weather days.

Guests might also notice no trolleys or horses are making their way through World Bazaar. But as at Walt Disney

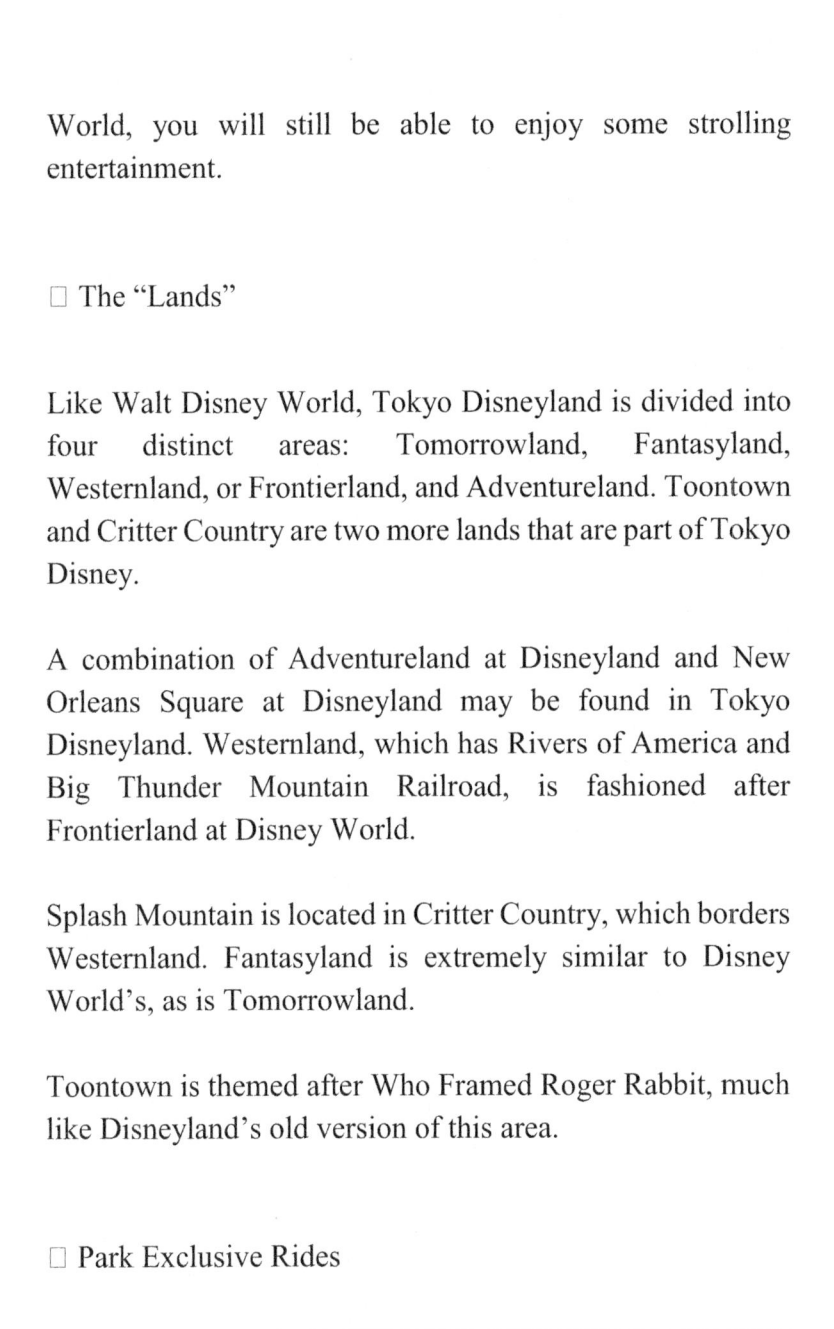

World, you will still be able to enjoy some strolling entertainment.

☐ The "Lands"

Like Walt Disney World, Tokyo Disneyland is divided into four distinct areas: Tomorrowland, Fantasyland, Westernland, or Frontierland, and Adventureland. Toontown and Critter Country are two more lands that are part of Tokyo Disney.

A combination of Adventureland at Disneyland and New Orleans Square at Disneyland may be found in Tokyo Disneyland. Westernland, which has Rivers of America and Big Thunder Mountain Railroad, is fashioned after Frontierland at Disney World.

Splash Mountain is located in Critter Country, which borders Westernland. Fantasyland is extremely similar to Disney World's, as is Tomorrowland.

Toontown is themed after Who Framed Roger Rabbit, much like Disneyland's old version of this area.

☐ Park Exclusive Rides

Several popular Disney rides, including Buzz Lightyear, Space Ranger Spin, Splash Mountain, Space Mountain, Pirates of the Caribbean, and Haunted Mansion, are available at Tokyo Disneyland.

These attractions typically just contain minor differences from their American counterparts and are in general very similar.

There are some unique attractions at Tokyo Disneyland that you won't find anywhere else. These are Pooh's Hunny Hunt, Monsters Inc. Enchanted Tale of Beauty and the Beast and Ride & Go Seek.

Enchanted Tale of Beauty and the Beast is the newest attraction to Tokyo Disneyland. Using cutting-edge special effects and technology, this attraction is a trackless dark ride that tells the tale of Beauty and the Beast.

Parades and Shows

Tokyo Disneyland is very well known for its parades and shows. Tokyo Disneyland's parades change frequently and seasonally. Currently, Disney Harmony in Color is parading throughout the park once a day while Tokyo Disneyland Electrical Parade runs nightly. Sky Full of Colors is a fireworks spectacular that runs nightly at 8:30 pm.

To the entertainment of visitors, additional live stage performances are presented throughout the parks. Shows like Mickey's Magical Music World in Fantasyland and Club Mouse Beat in Tomorrowland are in general very similar.

In a nutshell, Tokyo Disneyland is a wonderful experience for guests who have visited other Disney Parks or guests who are visiting their first park.

Tokyo Disneyland: Unlocking the Secrets to Japan's Happiest Place

Chapter 8

Tokyo Disney Resort Popular Theme Areas

Tokyo Disney Resort is home to two theme parks (Disneyland and DisneySea). Both theme parks are made up of seven different themed areas each, and two days are enough to explore all 14 of them.

In this chapter, we bring to you all the information you need to know about both theme park areas.

Now let's familiarize ourselves with the 7 themed areas of Disneyland, which include;

☐ The World Bazaar - A dining and shopping area modeled after a retro American town. Remember to stop by this shopping arcade before you leave, so you can pick up some souvenirs to take home.

☐ Tomorrowland - If you are interested in all things outer space and tomorrow's technology then visiting Tomorrowland is a must. A hive of futuristic and spacefaring technologies.

☐ Toontown - This is home to notable toon characters like Mickey Mouse, Minnie, Donald Duck, and Chip N Dale. In this suburban neighborhood, you'll find how Disney characters live, walk, and play inside their houses. There's even a kiddie roller-coaster for the little kids.

☐ Fantasyland - What's a visit to Tokyo Disneyland without seeing the famous Cinderella's Castle? Head over to Fantasyland to see the trademarked palace. Fantasyland is home to classic films, Beauty and the Beast, Snow White, and Peter Pan. Looking for that whimsical '' it's a small world" ride? This is the place to go.

☐ Critter Country - A haven for Brer rabbits and their friends. It is a land-based on the Disney film Song of the South. This is the zone of the Splash Mountain ride. The other ride in this zone is the Beaver Brothers Explorer Canoes, where you can freely float on a can Big Thunder awaits you!

☐ Westernland - Visit here if you want a whiff of Uncle Sam. This area is Tokyo's version of Frontierland and its home to Big Thunder Mountain and Tom Sawyer Island. Other rides that you'll find here include Country Bear Theater, The Diamond Horseshoe, and the Horseshoe Roundup.

☐ Adventureland - This is where you'll find the Swiss Family Treehouse and the Pirates of the Caribbean. As the name implies, this themed land takes you on crazy adventures in tropical jungles, Arabian bazaars, and the wild seas of the Caribbean.

Tokyo DisneySea Themed Ports include;

☐ Mediterranean Harbor - Mediterranean Harbor at the entrance to the park is styled after an Italian port town. Its buildings comprise the Tokyo DisneySea Hotel MiraCosta, and its shoreline boasts gondolas and canals in the style of Venice. Every day at the harbor, there are big exhibitions with boats and water fountains.

☐ Mysterious Island - Mysterious Island is found within the volcano at the heart of the park and is a page from the science fiction writings of Jules Verne. Here you can explore the depths of the ocean aboard one of Captain Nemo's submarines or journey to the center of the earth in one of his science vehicles.

☐ Mermaid Lagoon - Mermaid Lagoon allows surface dwellers to enter the undersea world of Ariel and her fishy friends from The Little Mermaid. Suitable for younger kids, this fanciful section of the park features rides and entertainment.

☐ Arabian Coast - The Arabian Coast recreates the world of Aladdin and 1001 Arabian Nights. Here, you can accompany Sinbad on his voyage of exploration or enjoy a magic show performed by Genie.

☐ Lost River Delta - The Lost River Delta was built among the ruins of an ancient temple pyramid in the Central American jungle. The Indiana Jones Adventure roller coaster descends into the ruins of a temple, and the Raging Spirits Roller Coaster thunders past next door. The port is where the Tokyo DisneySea Transit Steamers stop so they can move between the park's various areas.

☐ Port Discovery - Port Discovery is the marina of the future where visitors can check out the Searider, a simulation ride exploring the marine life with Nemo and Dory, go take a ride on one of the self-guided, experimental watercrafts that shuttles between the Aquatopia attraction's rocks, fountains, and whirlpools.

☐ American Waterfront - The American Waterfront zone is styled after the 20th-century harbor towns found around New York, New England, and Cape Cod. There's an elevated train, stores and restaurants in the American style, a playhouse, and the S.S. Columbia steamship with a lounge and restaurant on board. It is also home to the Tower of Terror ride.

Chapter 9

Exploring The Parks Best Rides

Both parks include somewhat modified versions of their US counterparts in addition to unique attractions not available at any other Disney Park. To enjoy the finest of Tokyo Disney Resort, make it a priority to ride these attractions!

Tokyo Disneyland and Tokyo DisneySea no longer offer FastPass. StandbyPass, Entry Request, and Disney Premier Access have replaced FastPass. All of which can be downloaded from the Disney Resort App.

Now let's continue...

Tokyo Disney Resort is a place of magical adventures and thrilling rides, where dreams come true and childhood memories come alive.

But with so many attractions at your disposal, where do you even start?

Well, buckle up because I'm about to whisk you away on a whirlwind tour of the best rides Tokyo Disney Resort has to offer.

Here's what you need to know before we move further.

The most visited Tokyo Disneyland attraction is Enchanted Tale of Beauty and the Beast. Make sure to start your morning ride with this one. Afterward, head to Pooh's Hunny Hunt. Take your time on these two enjoyable, trackless nighttime rides.

According to a recent 2023 questionnaire, the most visited attractions in Tokyo DisneySea include; Sindbad's Storybook Voyage, Toy Story Mania, Tower of Terror, and Journey to the Center of the Earth.

Tip: Use Disney Premier Access to skip the lines at some of the more popular rides.

Let's dive into it...

For Thrill-Seekers

☐ Space Mountain (closing in 2024) - A futurist roller coaster and a staple of Disney theme parks. Blast off on a high-speed rocket coaster through a dazzling cosmic tunnel. Prepare for drops, twists, and turns that will leave your heart racing and your mind in awe.

☐ Big Thunder Mountain Railroad - A mine and train - theme roller-coaster, modeled after its counterparts at Disneyland California, Disneyland Park Paris, and Disney World in Orlando, Florida.

Embark on a runaway mine train adventure through a wild western canyon. Brace yourself for geysers, waterfalls, and a runaway mine cart that'll have you screaming with laughter (and maybe a little fear).

☐ Pooh's Hunted Hunt - This one right is unique only to Tokyo Disneyland as you won't find it anywhere else. This trackless dark ride takes you on a whimsical journey through Pooh's Hundred Acre Wood, encountering heffalumps and woozles along the way. It's a delightful blend of charm and thrills, perfect for all ages.

☐ Journey to the Center of the Earth: Plunge into Mount Prometheus on a volcano exploration with freefalls, lava flows, and an epic finale.

☐ Tower of Terror: This classic freefall drop ride takes you on a chilling journey through the Hollywood Hotel with a new, original story just for Tokyo DisneySea.

☐ Raging Spirits: Hold on tight as you race through swirling tracks on this high-speed roller coaster with inversions and drops.

☐ Indiana Jones Adventure: Temple of the Crystal Skull: Navigate booby traps and perilous situations on this thrilling jeep ride through a mysterious temple.

For Fantasy Fans

☐ Enchanted Tale of Beauty and the Beast - Step into the magical world of Beauty and the Beast, reliving the classic story in a stunning immersive experience. Be our guest in the Beast's castle, waltz through the ballroom, and witness the heartwarming transformation firsthand.

☐ Monsters, Inc. Ride and Go Seek! - A dark ride attraction based on the 2001 film. Join Mike and Sulley on a hilarious interactive adventure through the Monstropolis factory. Help collect cans for Boo, avoid Roz's watchful eye, and blast through doors on this energetic dark ride.

☐ Peter Pan's Flight - Soar through the skies over Neverland, past twinkling stars and playful pirates, on this classic suspended dark ride. It's a timeless adventure that will have you believing in pixie dust all over again.

☐ Buzz Lightyear's Astro Blasters -
To infinity and beyond! Based on the Toy Story film franchise, this is an interactive shooting ride.

☐ Star Tours: The Adventure Continues -
You will travel back in time to a distant galaxy with this 3D motion simulator attraction.

For The Whole Family

☐ Pirates of the Caribbean - Sail the high seas with Captain Jack Sparrow on this swashbuckling boat ride. Encounter cursed pirates, explosive battles, and thrilling drops that will leave you feeling like a true buccaneer.

☐ Haunted Mansion - Take a spooky tour through a haunted mansion filled with mischievous ghosts and playful ghouls.

This classic dark ride is sure to delight and frighten in equal measure, making it a favorite for all ages.

☐ It's a Small World - Sing along to the iconic song as you embark on a heartwarming journey through a miniature world celebrating children from all over the globe. This cheerful boat ride is a delightful reminder of our shared humanity and the beauty of diversity.

☐ Sindbad's Storybook Voyage: Sail the Seven Seas with Sindbad on a gentle boat ride through vibrant scenes from his adventures.

☐ Toy Story Mania: Grab your laser guns and help Buzz Lightyear defeat Zurg in this interactive carnival game.

☐ Turtle Talk with Crush: Have a hilarious conversation with Crush from Finding Nemo in this interactive show using real-time animation.

☐ Jasmine's Flying Carpets: Soar through the skies on magic carpets above Agrabah, enjoying breathtaking views of the Arabian Coast.

Enchanted Adventures

☐ 20,000 Leagues Under the Sea: Dive into the underwater world of Atlantis with Captain Nemo on this submarine voyage.

☐ Fortress Explorations: Explore this interactive island full of hidden passages, shipwrecks, and a mysterious planetarium.

☐ Mystic Manor: Join Lord Henry Mystic on a whimsical adventure through his haunted mansion filled with magical artifacts.

☐ Journey with Duffy: Follow Duffy the Disney bear on a heartwarming boat ride through a fantastical world filled with his friends.

So grab your Mickey ears, get ready for an unforgettable adventure, and let the magic of Tokyo Disney whisk you away!

Which ride will you conquer first? I'm excited to hear about your magical journey!

Chapter 10

FANTASY SPRINGS

Like Fantasyland, Tokyo DisneySea's Fantasy Springs is a planned themed port (region).

The port draws inspiration from a mystical spring that opens a Disney Fantasy realm.

The new region, which marks the biggest expansion ever at Tokyo Disney Resort, promises to transport visitors to the magical worlds of Peter Pan, Tangled, and Frozen.

In addition to these four new attractions, the expansion will also add three restaurants, one shop and a new luxury hotel situated inside the port to Tokyo DisneySea.

The massive expansion, which will be the park's eighth stop, will have four attractions such as restaurants, stores, and a five-star hotel with a view of Tokyo DisneySea that is rumored to be the deluxe lodging at Tokyo Disney Resort!

Fantasy Springs Overview

The Oriental Land Company has announced that Fantasy Springs will open to guests on June 6, 2024!

The project's original opening date of 2023 was postponed because of the Covid-19 pandemic. The project is set to cost ¥320 billion (about $2.1 billion USD), and will be the Park's largest expansion, clocking in at approximately 140,000 square meters.

The Fantasy Springs addition is situated in what was once a parking lot between Tokyo DisneySea and Tokyo Disneyland, and it is connected to both the Arabian Coast and the Lost River Delta via a tunnel.

Accessing Fantasy Springs

Together with a valid Tokyo DisneySea Park ticket, visitors must have a Standby Pass or Disney Premier Access to enter Fantasy Springs at a designated time.

To experience the four attractions within Fantasy Springs, guests must obtain a Standby Bypass (free) or Disney Premier Access (paid) via the official Tokyo Disney Resort App.

Standby Pass can be obtained from the Tokyo Disney Resort app after entering the park, allowing guests to choose a time to visit the attraction.

The entire Frozen, Rapunzel's Lantern Festival, and Peter Pan's Neverland Adventure will be accessible with Disney Premier Access. At the same moment, Fairy Tinkerbell's Busy Buggy is exclusively accessible via the Stand Bypass.

Fantasy Springs Entrance

Passing via a recently constructed trail that connects the Arabian Coast with the Lost River Delta, visitors will first come across enchanted rock formations and springs that honor cherished Disney classics before being whisked away to the enchanted realms of Frozen, Tangled, and Peter Pan.

The springs will be enchanted with a stunning bioluminescence glow once dusk falls, thanks to an amazing lighting setup.

Tokyo DisneySea Fantasy Springs Hotel

The Tokyo DisneySea Fantasy Springs Hotel is a park-integrated Disney hotel that is located inside the park, following in the footsteps of Hotel MiraCosta.

There will be two restaurants, a lounge, and Fantasy Springs Gifts, a gift shop, within the exquisite 475-room hotel.

The Fantasy Chateau and the Grand Chateau are the two structures that make up the hotel. The Fantasy Chateau offers "deluxe type" rooms decorated with the flora and fauna of Fantasy Springs, while the Grand Chateau promises the most luxurious accommodation available at Tokyo Disney Resort.

There will be a mix of rooms with and without park views available at the hotel.

Tokyo DisneySea Fantasy Springs Hotel Pricing

The two buildings are offered at various pricing points:

Fantasy Chateau: Rooms start at ¥63,500 ($430 USD) per night.

Grand Chateau: Rooms start at ¥300,000 ($2300 USD) per night.

These are sample prices and vary depending on availability and time of year. Compared to the Fantasy Chateau, the Grand Chateau has a lot more benefits.

There is a dedicated entrance for hotel guests that leads straight to Fantasy Springs. There will also be a special park ticket available.

Chapter 11

TOKYO DISNEY SPECIAL SHOWS AND PARADES

They're like dazzling sprinkles on top of the already magical cake, adding bursts of music, color, and Disney charm to your day. These are a few of the most well-liked ones that you must not miss:

Parades;

Disney Harmony in Color (NEW) - This vibrant parade celebrates the beauty of diversity and friendship, featuring characters from classic and new Disney films in colorful costumes and energetic dance routines.

It became available from the 15th of April 2023.

Mickey Mouse and his Disney pals, including those from Coco by Disney and Pixar and Zootopia by Walt Disney Animation Studios, will also be there.

Location: Parade Route.
Duration: About 45 minutes (Performances: 1 daily).
Presented by NTT DOCOMO, Inc.

Apart from the locations accessible without prior reservations, there will also be specific viewing spaces reserved for guests with Disney Premier Access or Tokyo Disney Resort Vacation Package reservations.

Minnie @Funderland - Starting from January 10th to March 19th, 2024, join Minnie Mouse for a playful party parade filled with confetti, dancing, and surprises! Expect upbeat music, adorable costumes, and plenty of Minnie's signature sass.

Duration: About 35 minutes (2-3 performances daily).
Location: Parkview (Parade Route and Castle Forecourt).

With Disney Premier Access (charges apply), you can also enjoy it from designated viewing areas.

Dreaming Up! - This daytime parade is a breathtaking spectacle of floats adorned with intricate details, featuring iconic Disney characters like Mickey, Donald, and Cinderella. Prepare to be swept away by the enchanting music and dazzling costumes.

Duration: 35 minutes (1 performance daily).
Presented by: Disney characters.
No special entry qualification.

Tokyo Disneyland Electrical Parade Dream Lights - As twilight settles, this nighttime parade illuminates the park with over a million twinkling lights. Witness classic Disney scenes brought to life with moving floats, whimsical music, and a touch of nostalgia.

Duration: 45 minutes (1 performance daily).
Presented by: BIPOGY

Viewing Areas for Parades

There will be certain viewing places reserved for guests with Disney Premier Access or reservations for Tokyo Disney Resort vacation packages, in addition to those that don't require reservations in advance.

Shows

Very Minnie Remix - Immerse yourself in a high-energy celebration of past Tokyo Disneyland entertainment! This show features medleys of classic Disney tunes, stunning dance routines, and appearances by your favorite Disney characters.

Duration: 25 minutes, 2-3 times daily.

Presented by: Disney characters

No special qualification.

Let's Celebrate with Colors - Get ready to sing and dance along with Mickey, Minnie, and friends in this interactive show celebrating friendship and joy. Expect colorful costumes, catchy tunes, and an irresistible urge to join the party!

Duration: 25 minutes, 3-4 performances daily.
Presented by: Disney characters.

No special entry qualification is required.

Jamboree Mickey! Let's Dance! - Get your little ones up and moving with Mickey Mouse in this fun and interactive show. Sing along to familiar Disney songs, participate in games, and watch their faces light up with excitement.

Location: Adventureland (Theater Orleans)

Duration: 15 minutes (3-5 times a day).
Presented by: Mickey and friends.

Filling out an Entry Request on the Tokyo Disney Resort App while inside the park is necessary for this entertainment activity. If an entry request has been made and a time slot has been assigned, you will be able to access the venue.

One Man's Dream II - The Magic Lives On: This heartwarming stage show takes you on a journey through Walt Disney's life and legacy. Prepare to be inspired by his creativity, dedication, and passion for storytelling.

Duration: 45 minutes, 2 performances daily.
Presented by narrators and performers.

Mickey's PhilharMagic: This hilarious 4D adventure combines classic Disney animation with special effects, leaving you laughing, gasping, and tapping your toes.

Duration: 12 minutes, multiple performances daily.
No special entry qualification.
Presented by Donald Duck and Mickey Mouse).

Shows At Disneysea;

Harbors and Shores:

BraviSEAmo: Set sail on a journey across the Seven Seas with vibrant costumes, music, and acrobatics featuring Disney characters like Ariel, Ursula, and Miguel. Expect high-energy dancing, aerial stunts, and breathtaking water effects.

Mickey and Minnie's Big Band Beat: Swing into a roaring 1930s atmosphere with Mickey, Minnie, and friends. Tap your feet to classic Disney tunes, marvel at dazzling costumes, and witness energetic tap-dancing routines.

Legend of Mythica: Witness breathtaking performances by mythical creatures like mermaids, centaurs, and griffins in this mesmerizing water show. Be captivated by synchronized swimming, synchronized diving, and dazzling effects brought to life by projected illusions.

Mysterious Islands and Mystical Lands:

Out of Shadowland: Embark on a mystical journey through the Lost River Delta with Mickey, Minnie, and friends.

Encounter eerie spirits, and brave jungle perils, and discover the power of friendship and light. Expect captivating special effects, puppetry, and haunting melodies.

Mystic Rhythms: Step into a vibrant celebration of the African savanna with this dynamic show. Feel the beat of drums, witness acrobatic dances, and admire dazzling costumes inspired by animal patterns. Prepare for an energetic and uplifting experience.

Lost Continent and Magical Realms:

Fantasmic! Witness a spectacular showdown between Mickey and the forces of darkness in this nighttime masterpiece. Be mesmerized by water jets, lasers, fireworks, and projections on a giant water screen. Expect iconic Disney scenes, classic characters, and a breathtaking display of light and magic. Featuring stunning water effects, projections, fireworks, and iconic Disney characters. Stay tuned for its grand return!

Duration: approx. 25 minutes, 1 performance daily
No special entry qualification.
Presented by: Disney characters

Parades:

Disney Sea Shimmering Dreams: Sail into a vibrant parade showcasing Disney characters from across the Seven Seas. Watch Ariel splash through on a seashell chariot, let Moana glide by on a canoe, and sing along to familiar Disney tunes.

Tokyo DisneySea Electrical Parade
Dream Lights: As twilight descends, immerse yourself in a dazzling spectacle of illuminated floats featuring classic Disney scenes and characters. Witness hundreds of thousands of twinkling lights dancing to beloved Disney melodies.

To end with, depending on the weather or other conditions on your day of visit, the location of each viewing area is subject to change. For information, please speak with a cast member on the day of your visit.

Important Note: Entry qualifications for certain shows might change in the future, so it's always best to check the official Tokyo Disneyland website or app for the latest information before your visit. Enjoy your magical adventure!

Beyond the parks

My recommendations for things to do in and around Tokyo!

Make time for a day at Sanrio Puroland, a Hello Kitty theme park, and an afternoon at TeamLab Planets TOKYO, a well-liked attraction. Utilize the easy hop-on-hop-off bus to explore Tokyo.

Spend a rainy afternoon inside Japan's largest indoor theme park, Tokyo Joypolis, near Tokyo Disney!

Venturing Beyond the Disney Magic: Nearby Tokyo Delights

While Tokyo Disney Resort offers endless enchantment, venturing beyond its gates opens a treasure trove of diverse experiences. Here's a glimpse into three popular nearby attractions:

Tokyo Tower:

- Soaring Symbol: Rising 333 meters above the city, Tokyo Tower is an iconic landmark offering panoramic views of the sprawling metropolis. Enjoy breathtaking vistas from the main observation deck or ascend to the topmost Special Observation Deck for an even more exhilarating experience.

- Illuminated Wonder: As twilight settles, the tower transforms into a dazzling beacon, its orange and white lights painting the cityscape in a vibrant glow. Witness enchanting light shows on special occasions, adding another layer of magic to your evening.

- Retro Charm: Step back in time at the base of the tower, where quirky cafes and retro shops evoke a nostalgic atmosphere. Browse vintage finds, savor Japanese classics like taiyaki (fish-shaped pastries), and soak in the unique charm of old-world Tokyo.

Sensoji Temple:

- Spiritual Heart: Immerse yourself in the ancient traditions of Japan at Sensoji Temple, the oldest temple in Tokyo. Explore the vibrant Nakamise market, lined with stalls selling traditional crafts and souvenirs, before entering the temple grounds.

- Serene Tranquility: Witness the rituals and practices of Buddhist monks, marvel at the ornate architecture, and soak in the peaceful atmosphere. Light incense sticks, write a wish on a prayer strip, and experience the serenity of this treasured cultural landmark.

- Hidden Delights: Explore the surrounding Asakusa district, bustling with traditional restaurants, teahouses, and rickshaw tours. Discover hidden alleys showcasing exquisite craftsmanship, sample local delicacies like Sensoji temple melon-pan (sweet bread) and lose yourself in the vibrant pulse of old Tokyo.

Yokohama:

- Modern Metropolis: Take a short train ride to Yokohama, a futuristic city bursting with contemporary architecture, trendy neighborhoods, and exciting attractions. Marvel at the Yokohama Landmark Tower, explore the Minato Mirai waterfront district and discover hidden gems like the Ramen Museum.

- Culinary Adventure: Embark on a culinary journey through Yokohama's diverse food scene. Sample fresh seafood at the bustling Minato Osakana Base, indulge in international cuisines at Yokohama

Chinatown or savor regional specialties like Yokohama curry rice.

- Thrilling Adventures: Get your adrenaline pumping at Yokohama Cosmo World, an amusement park featuring roller coasters, a Ferris wheel, and exhilarating rides. Experience the thrill of speed at Nissan Motor Studio or delve into the world of maritime history at the Yokohama Minato Museum.

Whether you're seeking cultural immersion, modern delights, or thrilling adventures, venturing beyond the Disney gates promises an unforgettable experience. So, pack your curiosity, lace up your walking shoes, and prepare to discover the vibrant tapestry that is Tokyo!

Ikspiari

Ikspiari, situated at the gateway to Tokyo Disney Resort, is a dazzling haven of shopping, dining, and entertainment that extends the Disney magic beyond the park gates. Imagine a charming town infused with Disney flair, where every corner offers something to captivate your senses.

Shopping Adventures:

- Disney Treasures: Dive into a wonderland of official Disney merchandise. From classic Mickey ears to movie-themed apparel, find collectibles, toys, and souvenirs for every Disney fan.

- Global Brands: Indulge in international fashion and lifestyle brands like Guess, Lush, and Tommy Hilfiger, alongside popular Japanese retailers like Daiso, a treasure trove of discount finds.

- Themed Delights: Discover boutiques inspired by Disney movies like Pirates of the Caribbean and Alice in Wonderland. Pick up unique souvenirs and apparel that evoke the spirit of your favorite Disney stories.

Culinary Delights:

- Restaurant Extravaganza: Embark on a global culinary journey with over 130 restaurants catering to diverse palates. Sample Italian pasta, savor Japanese ramen, or indulge in American-style burgers and BBQ.

- Disney-Themed Treats: Fuel your fun with themed snacks and sweet treats. Sip on a Mickey Mouse latte, munch on Minnie-shaped cookies, or savor a delectable meal at the Crystal Palace, inspired by Cinderella's castle.

- Cozy Cafes and Bars: Relax and unwind at charming cafes and bars. Sip on a specialty coffee, enjoy a glass of wine, or unwind with a refreshing cocktail after a day of shopping and sightseeing.

Entertainment Galore:

- Cinema Ikspiari: Catch the latest blockbusters and Disney classics at this state-of-the-art movie theater boasting 16 screens and IMAX technology.

- Live Shows and Events: Immerse yourself in captivating live performances, from magic shows and musicals to themed parades and character meet-and-greets.

- Game Center: Challenge your friends and family to classic arcade games and thrilling virtual reality experiences.

More Than Just Shopping:

Ikspiari offers a vibrant atmosphere throughout the day. Stroll through beautiful, themed areas, marvel at dazzling illuminations in the evening, and let the Disney magic seep into your experience.

Whether you're a die-hard Disney fan or simply seeking a unique shopping and entertainment experience, Ikspiari promises a delightful escape with something for everyone. So, pack your bags, unleash your inner child, and get ready to immerse yourself in the captivating world of Ikspiari!

Explore, let your imagination take flight, and discover the enchanting world beyond the shows!

How to Optimize Your Tokyo Disneyland Trip

Okay! Now that you've been updated to the modalities at Disney Resort, let's get tips on how to optimize your time in Tokyo Disney!
As soon as you enter the park, you need to carry out the following actions:

1. Download the Tokyo Disney Resort App and add your tickets to the app – As I mentioned earlier, this should be the VERY FIRST thing you do when you get to the park. You will be able to control the group's total amount of priority passes and premier access by doing this. During your vacation, it will also help you with other administrative tasks like making restaurant reservations and checking ride wait times.

2. Purchase Disney Premier Access for Beauty and the Beast - As soon as you arrive at the park, you should buy the pass because this attraction is very popular. Unless you don't mind waiting in line for the trip, which could take two to four hours depending on the volume of people that day.

3. If you can, use Priority Pass to ride the most popular ride first. At Tokyo Disneyland, for instance, Space Mountain is one of the most well-liked rides. If a Priority Pass is available, take it right away. After two hours, obtain another Priority Pass for more attractions.

4. Check the wait times for other rides: As I mentioned earlier, one of the things you should do as soon as you arrive at the park is use the Disneyland app's map to view the wait times for each ride. You should verify the current status of the rides as some may be closed for maintenance. Then, begin strategizing!

5. Find out which Tokyo Disneyland ride is the most appreciated. Purchasing passes for the following rides should be your top priority because they are more popular than the others:

Enchanted Tales of Beauty and the Beast

Splash Mountain

Monsters, Inc. Ride & Go Seek
Buzz Lightyear's Astro Blasters

Space Mountain

Big Thunder Mountain

Haunted Mansion

Pooh's Hunny Hunt

6. Check for the park's special parades – During the peak period, there are many parades a day. For example, when I visited at Easter there were at least 3 parades on the day I

went. Moving around the park is a little challenging during these parades because the main roadways are closed. So, remember to keep this in mind!

Also, if you visit around a holiday like Christmas (when there will certainly be a Christmas parade), the park will be closed during the parade due to high demand—people would often "reserve" their spots starting early in the morning.

7. Don't forget about the daily fireworks! This usually happens around 8 to 8:30 PM so try to stay at the park as long as you can to witness this firework show.

8. Take advantage of the rider switch: Parents with young children can take turns riding while the other waits with the child.

9. Pack for the weather: Be prepared for rain or hot sun depending on the season.

10. Remember to have fun! Lastly, although I realize this is a lot, making the most of your Disneyland stay may be demanding. It's okay if you were unable to board the ride you had intended! Despite not being able to ride Beauty and the Beast on my three visits to Tokyo Disneyland, I still had a great experience. And honestly, that's all that matters right?

Tokyo Disneyland: Unlocking the Secrets to Japan's Happiest Place

Chapter 12

GUESTS WITH DISABILITIES

Tokyo Disneyland provides accommodations for people with developmental disabilities, dietary restrictions, and impairments in hearing, vision, and mobility.

The park also welcomes service animals and does its best to support people with other kinds of conditions.

To secure assistance from park employees, guests are encouraged to apply for a "Guest Assistance Card" upon arriving at the park. While most applications are successful, it is important to note that the park may refuse any applications from guests without a Japanese disability passbook.

The official Tokyo Disneyland website has more details about the park's accessibility for visitors. Additionally, they can use an online form to obtain information on park accessibility.

Barrier-free environment

Tokyo Disneyland is relatively barrier-free. While some areas of the park feature dirt roads and cobblestone pathways that may inconvenience individuals with mobility impairments, those areas can be navigated via alternative routes.

Most of the park's attractions are accessible without requiring stairs, and it also has a large number of accessible restrooms. Benches and rest areas are strewn throughout the park, as are drinking fountains, food vendors, and storage lockers.

Braille and sign language services are available throughout the park, but only to individuals familiar with their Japanese versions. It should be noted that a lot of the park's attractions change concerning temperature, humidity, sound, and lighting. For additional information, see the park's website.

Assistive technologies

Tokyo Disneyland allows its guests to bring their own mobility devices into the park. But to enter the rides, visitors have to move to wheelchairs provided by the park. There are three types of wheelchairs provided by parks: manual, motor-assisted, and electric.

They can be rented from a station outside the park or borrowed on a ride-by-ride basis inside the park proper. It is important to note that Tokyo Disneyland does not always support visitors who require assistance getting into and out of park-issued chairs.

The park also reserves the right to refuse guests entry to any attraction if they believe that a guest's safety is at risk. Every of the park's gift shops and accessory businesses are wheelchair accessible thanks to their wide doorways and ramps.

Some parades and shows are accessible to nearly everyone regardless of their physical or cognitive status, while others are all but closed off to persons with disabilities. It is recommended that guests visit Tokyo Disneyland's website in advance to review the rules of each attraction.

Tokyo Disney Resort's Disability Access Service (DAS) Explained

The Disability Access Service (DAS) at Tokyo Disney Resort aims to provide guests with accessibility needs a fulfilling and comfortable park experience.

It allows them to avoid waiting in regular lines for most attractions by offering alternative solutions.

Who is eligible for a DAS pass at Tokyo Disney Resort?

The official guidelines state that the DAS is intended for guests with the following:

- Physical disabilities: This includes those with mobility impairments, limited stamina, or difficulty standing for extended periods.

- Developmental disabilities: This includes guests with autism spectrum disorder, intellectual disabilities, or sensory processing disorders.

- Neurological disabilities: This includes guests with epilepsy, chronic pain, or other neurological conditions that may hinder waiting in line.

- Cognitive disabilities: This includes guests with memory impairments or learning disabilities that may make queuing difficult.

- Expectant mothers: While not explicitly stated, some pregnant women may also be eligible for DAS if they experience health concerns associated with standing for long periods.

It's important to note that:

- An official disability certificate or diagnosis is not always required but having one can expedite the process.

- Guests with hidden disabilities are also eligible for the DAS.

- Each case is assessed individually, and not all disabilities automatically qualify for the service.

How to use the DAS pass at Tokyo Disney Resort:

1. Register at Guest Relations: Visit the designated Guest Relations area with your park ticket and any available proof of disability.

2. Explain your needs and preferred alternatives: Discuss your limitations and preferred ways to access attractions with the Cast Member.

3. Schedule return times: You will be assigned specific return times for the attractions you choose.

4. Return at your designated time: Head to the designated entrance of the attraction at your assigned time and enjoy the ride!

Additional points to remember:

- DAS does not guarantee immediate access to attractions. Wait times may still apply depending on the chosen alternative access method.

- Not all attractions offer alternative access options.

- It's advised to plan your itinerary and prioritize the attractions you'd like to experience with DAS.

- Be patient and understanding as Cast Members work to accommodate your needs.

Does the DAS pass cost money?

There is no additional cost associated with obtaining or using a Disability Access Service (DAS) pass at Tokyo Disney Resort. Your regular park ticket grants you access to the DAS service alongside all the other park features and attractions.

The focus of the DAS is on providing equal access and ensuring a comfortable experience for guests with accessibility needs, not on adding extra fees. Remember, the service aims to cater to individuals who might struggle with traditional queuing and waiting lines, and charging for it would go against the spirit of inclusivity.

Overall, the DAS pass is a valuable service that allows guests with accessibility needs to experience the magic of Tokyo Disney Resort in a way that suits their abilities.

If you have any questions or require further assistance, don't hesitate to reach out to Cast Members at Guest Relations.

They are available to help you make the most of your Disney adventure!

CONCLUSION

Get ready for a rollercoaster of emotions – Tokyo Disney is coming for you!

From heart-pounding drops on Space Mountain to heartwarming tears during One Man's Dream, this park will leave you breathless.

Embrace the childlike wonder, share laughter with loved ones, and lose yourself in the stories, characters, and dreams that come alive within the park.

Be swept away by the vibrant costumes, captivated by the dazzling shows, and fueled by the contagious Disney magic.

But Tokyo Disneyland's magic isn't just about iconic rides and familiar faces.

It's about the way the air crackles with anticipation as you wait in line, the shared gasps and joyful screams that erupt from rollercoasters, and the whispered "I love you" to Mickey Mouse that leaves tears welling in your eyes. It's about the delicious aroma of freshly baked churros, the vibrant costumes that transport you to faraway lands, and the infectious laughter that spills over from families huddled together for the fireworks finale.

This isn't just a theme park; it's a portal to a world where imagination reigns supreme. It's a place where worries dissolve and dreams take flight, where families bond over shared memories, and where you can be anything you dream of being, even for just a day.

So, dear reader, I urge you: don't let the magic of Tokyo Disneyland remain a distant dream. Start planning your adventure today.

Pack your sense of wonder, dust off your Mickey's ears, and get ready to be swept away by a whirlwind of unforgettable memories.

Believe in the impossible, embrace the unexpected, and prepare to have your heart forever touched by the magic that lives within the gates of Tokyo Disneyland.

The adventure awaits. Are you ready?

Trust me, you'll leave Tokyo Disneyland with a smile wider than Mickey's and a heart overflowing with pixie dust. Now go forth and make some Tokyo Disneyland dreams come true!

Tokyo Disneyland: Unlocking the Secrets to Japan's Happiest Place

Printed in Great Britain
by Amazon